COMPUTER
ACRONYMS
&
ABBREVIATIONS

Compiled by

ELIE ALBALA

ALPEL PUBLISHING

Computer Acronyms and Abbreviations
Compiled by Elie Albala
Cartoon by paul gamboli

Published by
Alpel Publishing
P. O. Box 203, Chambly
Quebec, Canada J3L 4B3
Tel. (514) 658-6205
Fax (514) 658-3514

Canadian Cataloguing in Publication Data

Albala, Elie, 1942-

Computer Acronyms and Abbreviations:
Over 4000 entries and what they stand for

ISBN   0-921993-06-4

1. Computers–Acronyms. 2. Computers–Abbreviations. 3. Electronic data processing–Acronyms. 4. Electronic data processing–Abbreviations. I. Title.

QA76.15.A35 1992   004'.03   C92-090506-4

Printed in Canada

*To my Parents,
with love,
respect and gratitude.*

TO THE READER

This book contains over **4000 Computer Acronyms & Abbreviations** *and* **what they stand for.** *If you keep it within easy reach, you will find it helpful, informative and practical.*

Since it is my intention to periodically publish revised editions of this reference book, I'll be happy to receive any comments or suggestions as a result of its use.

Elie Albala

AA	Abbreviated Addressing
AA	Absolute Accuracy
AA	Absolute Address
AA	Absolute Altimeter
AA	Absolute Altitude
AA	Access Arm
AA	Acoustic Absorptivity
AA	Action Area
AA	Arithmetic Average
AAAI	American Association for Artificial Intelligence
AAAS	American Association for the Advancement of Science
AAC	Accompanying Audio Channel
AAC	Acoustical Attenuation Constant
AAC	Automatic Aperture Control
AACC	American Automatic Control Council
AACS	Advanced Automatic Compilation System
AADC	All-Application Digital Computer
AADS	Automatic Applications Development System
AAE	American Association of Engineers
AAEE	American Association of Electrical Engineers
AAES	American Association of Engineering Society
AAGR	Average Annual Growth Rate
AAIM	American Association of Industrial Management
AAIMS	An Analytical Information Management System
AAL	Absolute Assembly Language
AAL	Acoustic Absorption Loss
AAME	American Association of Microprocessor Engineers
AAO	Authorized Acquisition Objective
AAP	Analyst Assistance Program
AAP	Associative Array Processor
AAP	Attached Applications Processor
AARS	Automatic Address Recognition Subsystem
AAS	Advanced Administrative System
AAS	Automatic Addressing System
AAU	Address Arithmetic Unit
AAVD	Automatic Alternate Voice Data
AB	Acetate Base
AB	Address Bus
ABA	American Bankers Association
ABAC	Association of Business and Administrative Computing
ABB	Array of Building Blocks
abbrev	Abbreviation
ABC	Approach By Concept

ABC	**Automatic Bass Compensation**
ABCS	**Automatic Base Communication Systems**
ABDL	**Automatic Binary Data Link**
ABE	**Arithmetic Building Element**
ABEND	**Abnormal End**
ABFD	**Affordable Basic Floppy Disk**
ABL	**Accepted Batch Listing**
ABL	**Automatic Bootstrap Loader**
ABLP	**Air Bearing Lift Pad**
ABM	**Asynchronous Balanced Mode**
ABM	**Automated Batch Mixing**
ABMPS	**Automated Business Mail Processing System**
ABP	**Actual Block Processor**
abr	**Abridged**
abs	**Absolute**
AC	**Absolute Coding**
AC	**Absorption Circuit**
AC	**Absorption Coefficient**
AC	**Absorption Control**
AC	**Absorption Current**
AC	**Acceptor Circuit**
AC	**Acoustic Clarifier**
AC	**Acoustic Compliance**
AC	**Acoustic Coupler**
AC	**Active Circuit**
AC	**Active Component**
AC	**Active Computer**
AC	**Active Current**
AC	**Actual Count**
AC	**Adaptive Communication**
AC	**Adaptive Control**
AC	**Address Characters**
AC	**Address Computation**
AC	**Adjusted Circuit**
AC	**Alignment Chart**
AC	**Alternating Current**
AC	**Analog Channel**
AC	**Analog Communications**
AC	**Analog Computer**
AC	**Automatic Computer**
AC	**Automatic Control**
ACA	**Asynchronous Communications Adaptor**
ACAP	**Advanced Computer for Array Processing**
ACB	**Access Control Block**
ACB	**Adapter Control Block**
ACB	**Application Control Block**
ACBS	**Accrediting Commission for Business Schools**
acc	**Accept**
acc	**Account**

acc	**Accumulate**
ACC	**Application Control Code**
ACCA	**Asynchronous Communications Control Attachment**
acce	**Acceptance**
acct	**Account**
accum	**Accumulator**
ACD	**Alternating Current Dump**
ACD	**Automatic Call Distributor**
ACE	**Audio Compression and Expansion**
ACE	**Automated Computing Engine**
ACE	**Automated Cost Estimating**
ACF	**Access Control Field**
ACF	**Advanced Communications Function**
ACH	**Automated Clearing Houses**
ACI	**Automatic Car Identification**
ACIA	**Asynchronous Communications Interface Adapter**
ACK	**Acknowledge Character**
ack	**Acknowledged**
ack	**Acknowledgment**
ACL	**Application Control Language**
ACM	**Association for Computing Machinery**
ACPA	**Association of Computer Programmers and Analysts**
ACR	**Address Control Register**
ACR	**Audio Cassette Recorder**
ACR	**Automatic Call Recording**
ACS	**Adaptive Control System**
ACS	**Advanced Communications Service**
ACS	**Application Customizer Service**
ACS	**Associated Computer System**
ACS	**Automatic Checkout System**
ACS	**Automatic Control System**
ACT	**Active Control Technology**
ACT	**Alternating Current Transmission**
ACT	**Analogical Circuit Technique**
ACT	**Automated Contingency Translator**
ACU	**Address Control Unit**
ACU	**Arithmetic Control Unit**
ACU	**Automatic Calling Unit**
ACUTE	**Accountants Computer Users Technical Exchange**
ACV	**Address Control Vector**
AD	**Abbreviated Dialing**
AD	**Absolute Delay**
AD	**Acetate Disc**
AD	**Acoustic Dispersion**
AD	**Active Decoder**
AD	**Active Device**
AD	**Adjusted Decibels**
AD	**Amplitude Distortion**
AD	**Analog Data**

AD	Authorized Distributor
ADA	Automatic Data Acquisition
ADAC	Automated Direct Analog Computer
ADAL	Action Data Automation Language
ADAM	Advanced Data Access Method
ADAM	Automatic Direct Access Management
ADAS	Automatic Disk Allocation System
ADB	Adjusted Debit Balance
ADC	Analog Digital Converter
ADC	Area Distribution Center
ADCCP	Advanced Data Communications Control Procedure
ADD	Amplitude Density Distribution
ADD	Automatic Document Distribution
ADDDS	Automatic Direct Distance Dialing System
ADDR	Address Register
addr	Address
ADDS	Advanced Data Display System
ADE	Automatic Data Entry
ADE	Automatic Design Engineering
ADE	Automatic Drafting Equipment
ADES	Automatic Digital Encoding System
ADF	Amplitude Distribution Function
ADF	Application Development Facility
ADF	Automatic Document Feeder
ADI	Alternating Direction Implicit
ADI	Alternating Direction Iterative
ADI	American Documentation Institute
ADI	Automatic Direction Indicator
adj	Adjective
ADL	Acoustic Delay Line
ADL	Amplifying Delay Line
ADL	Automatic Data Link
ADL	Automatic Data Logger
ADM	Activity Data Method
ADM	Adaptive Delta Modulation
admin	Administration
ADP	Automatic Data Processing
ADPE	Automatic Data Processing Equipment
ADPS	Automatic Data Processing System
ADPSO	Association of Data Processing Service Organizations
ADPT	Absolute Digital Position Transducer
adr	Address
adr	Addressing
ADR	Application Definition Record
ADR	Applied Data Research
ADS	Accurately Defined Systems
ADS	Activity Data Sheet
ADS	Advanced Debugging System
ADS	Analog Digital Subsystem

ADS	Automated Design System
ADT	Active Disk Table
ADT	Application Design Tool
ADT	Application-Dedicated Terminal
ADT	Attribute Distributed Tree
ADT	Automatic Detection and Tracking
ADU	Automatic Dial Unit
adv	Advice
adv	Advise
ADX	Automatic Data Exchange
AE	Absolute Efficiency
AE	Absolute Error
AE	Active Element
AE	Application Engineer
AEA	American Electronics Association
AEC	Architectural, Engineering and Construction
AED	Automated Engineering Design
AEDS	Association for Educational Data Systems
AEL	Audit Entry Language
AEN	Active Electric Network
AES	Audio Engineering Society
AES	Automatic Extraction System
AET	Acoustic Emission Testing
AET	Automatic Exchange Tester
AF	Acoustic Feedback
AF	Acoustic Filter
AF	Active Filter
AF	Address Field
AF	Amplification Factor
AF	Amplitude Fading
AF	Arithmetic Flag
AF	Aspect Factor
AF	Audio Frequency
AFC	Automatic Field Control
AFC	Automatic Frequency Control
AFCOM	Association For Computer Operations Managers
affil	Affiliated
AFI	Automatic Fault Isolation
AFIP	American Federation for Information Processing
AFM	Absorption Frequency Meter
AFM	Application Functions Module
AFO	Advanced File Organization
AFP	Automatic Floating Point
AFR	Amplitude-Frequency Response
AFR	Application Function Routine
AFT	Active File Table
AFT	Analog Facility Terminal
AFT	Automated Funds Transfer
AG	Abnormal Glow

AG	Address Generator
AG	Association Graph
agc	Agency
AGU	Address Generation Unit
AH	Absolute Humidity
AH	Acceptor Handshake
AHC	Ampere-Hour Capacity
AHM	Ampere-Hour Meter
AI	Absolute Instruction
AI	Acceptor Impurity
AI	Acoustic Intensity
AI	Artificial Intelligent
AIA	Aerospace Industries Association
AID	Acoustic Intrusion Detector
AID	Analog Interface Device
AID	Attention Identifier
AID	Automatic Information Distribution
AID	Automatic Interaction Detection
AIDS	Acoustic Intelligence Data System
AIDS	Advanced Interactive Debugging System
AIDS	Advanced Interactive Display System
AIDS	Automatic Illustrated Documentation System
AIDS	Automatic Inventory Dispatching System
AIEE	American Institute of Electrical Engineers
AIFF	Audio Interchange File Format
AIG	Address Indicating Group
AIIE	American Institute of Industrial Engineers
AIL	Arithmetic Input Left
AIM	Access Isolation Mechanism
AIM	Application Interface Module
AIM	Associative Index Method
AIM	Avalanche Induced Migration
AIMS	Automated Industry Management Services
AIP	Automated Imagery Processing
AIR	Acoustic Intercept Receiver
AIR	Arithmetic Input Right
AIS	Advanced Information Systems
AIS	Analog Input System
AIS	Automated Information System
AIS	Automatic Intercept System
AIT	Advanced Information Technology
AIU	Abstract Information Unit
AJ	Active Junction
AK	Accumulation Key
AKA	Also Known As
AL	Achromatic Lens
AL	Acoustic Lens
AL	Active Line
al	Alphabetic

AL	Assembler Language
AL	Assembly Language
ALB	Arithmetic and Logic Box
ALB	Assembly Line Balancing
ALC	Adaptive Logic Circuit
ALC	Assembly Language Coding
ALD	Advanced Logic Diagram
ALD	Automatic Logic Diagram
ALF	Application Library File
ALF	Automatic Line Feed
ALGOL	Algorithmic Oriented Language
ALL	Application Load List
ALLC	Association of Literary and Linguistic Computing
alloc	Allocation
ALM	Asynchronous Line Module
ALN	Attribute Level Number
ALP	Assembly Language Program
ALP	Automated Learning Process
ALPS	Advanced Linear Programming System
ALS	Advanced Logistics System
ALS	Amplitude Level Selection
ALS	Arithmetic Logic Section
ALT	Accelerated Life Test
alt	Alternate
ALT	Average Logistic Time
ALU	Arithmetic and Logical Unit
AM	Absentee Mode
AM	Absorption Modulation
AM	Access Method
AM	Access Mode
AM	Accompaniment Manual
AM	Acoustic Memory
AM	Acoustical Mode
AM	Address Mode
AM	Address Modifier
AM	Addressed Memory
AM	Amplitude Modulation
AM	Asynchronous Modem
AMA	Associative Memory Address
AMA	Associative Memory Array
AMA	Automated Message Accounting
amb	Ambassador
AMD	Associative Memory Data
AME	Automatic Monitoring Equipment
AME	Average Magnitude of Error
AMH	Application Message Handler
AMI	Average Mutual Information
AMIS	Automated Management Information System
AML	Amplitude Modulated Link

AML	Application Module Library
AMM	Analog Monitor Module
AMNL	Amplitude-Modulation Noise Level
AMO	Area Maintenance Office
amp	Ampere
amp	Amplifier
AMR	Absolute Maximum Rating
AMR	Absolute Minimum Resistance
AMR	Automatic Message Routing
AMS	American Mathematical Society
AMS	Application Management System
AMS	Asymmetric Multiprocessing System
AMS	Automated Maintenance System
AMSV	Absolute Maximum Supply Voltage
AMT	Advanced Manufacturing Technique
AMT	Advanced Manufacturing Technology
AMT	Automated Microfiche Terminal
AMU	Association of Minicomputer Users
AMW	Amplitude Modulated Wave
AN	Active Network
AN	Amplifier Noise
AN	Amplitude Noise
ANA	Automatic Network Analyzer
anal	Analysis
ANI	Automated Number Identification
ANL	Automatic New Line
anon	Anonymous
ANSI	American National Standards Institute
AO	Acoustical Ohm
AO	Automated Operation
AOI	Automated Operation Interface
AOL	Application Oriented Language
AOQ	Average Outgoing Quality
AOQL	Average Outgoing Quality Limit
AOS	Advanced Operating System
AOU	Arithmetic Output Unit
AOU	Associative Output Unit
AP	Abnormal Propagation
AP	Aborting Procedure
AP	Absolute Power
AP	Absolute Pressure
AP	Absolute Programming
AP	Acoustic Pickup
AP	Action Potential
AP	Actual Power
AP	Address Part
AP	Amplitude Permeability
AP	Application Program
AP	Argument Pointer

AP	Arithmetic Processor
AP	Array Processor
AP	Associative Processor
AP	Attached Processor
AP	Audio Processing
APA	Actual Parameter Area
APAR	Authorized Program Analysis Report
APB	Application Program Block
APC	Area Positive Control
APC	Associative Processor Control
APC	Automatic Peripheral Control
APC	Automatic Phase Control
APC	Automatic Potential Control
APD	Approach Progress Display
APE	Application Program Evaluation
APF	Authorized Program Facility
APG	Application Program Generator
APG	Automatic Priority Group
API	Application Program Interface
API	Automatic Priority Interrupt
APIS	Array Processing Instruction Set
APL	A Programming Language
APL	Algorithmic Programming Language
APL	Applied Physics Laboratory
APL	Automatic Program Load
APO	Automatic Power Off
APP	Advanced Procurement Plan
APP	Associative Parallel Processor
approx	Approximate
APPU	Application Program Preparation Utility
APR	Alternate Path Retry
APR	Automatic Passbook Recording
APS	Assembly Programming System
APSE	Ada Programming Support Environment
apt	Apartment
APT	Automatic Program Control
APT	Automatic Programming Tool
APU	Analog Processing Unit
APU	Arithmetic Processing Unit
APU	Asynchronous Processing Unit
APU	Auxiliary Power Unit
AQL	Acceptable Quality Level
AQS	Automated Quotation Systems
AR	Abnormal Reflections
AR	Accumulator Register
AR	Achieved Reliability
AR	Acoustic Reactance
AR	Acoustic Refraction
AR	Acoustic Resistance

AR	Acoustical Reflectivity
AR	Addition Record
AR	Address Register
AR	Adjustable Resistor
AR	Amplitude Range
AR	Amplitude Resonance
AR	Amplitude Response
AR	Arithmetic Register
AR	Associative Register
AR	Automated Register
AR	Automatic Restart
ARA	Attitude Reference Assembly
ARA	Automatic Route Advance
ARAT	Automatic Random Access Transport
arb	Arbitrary
ARC	Attached Resource Computer
arch	Architecture
ARCS	Automated Ring Code System
ARDD	Analysis Requiring Design and Development
ARF	Automatic Report Feature
arg	Argument
ARI	Applications Reference Index
ARI	Automated Readability Index
arith	Arithmetic
ARL	Average Run Length
ARM	Asynchronous Response Mode
ARM	Availability Reliability Maintainability
ARMM	Automatic Reliability Mathematical Model
ARO	After Receipt of Order
ARPA	Advanced Research Projects Agency
ARR	Address Recall Register
ARRL	American Radio Relay League
ART	Active Repair Time
ART	Automatic Request Transmission
ART	Average Run Time
art	Article
ARU	Audio Response Unit
AS	Absolute Scale
AS	Abstract Symbol
AS	Acceleration Switch
AS	Accepting Station
AS	Acoustic Shock
AS	Acoustic Suspension
AS	Active Systems
AS	Actuating System
AS	Address Syllable
AS	Amplitude Selection
AS	Amplitude Separator
ASA	Accelerated Storage Adapter

ASA	American Standards Association
ASA	American Statistical Association
ASA	Automatic Spectrum Analyzer
ASAP	As Soon As Possible
asbl	Assembler
ASC	Adaptive Speed Control
ASC	Associative Structure Computer
ASC	Automatic System Controller
ASCE	American Society of Civil Engineers
ASCII	American Standard Code for Information Interchange
ASID	Address Space Identifier
ASIS	American Society for Information Science
ASK	Amplitude Shift Keying
ASM	Auxiliary Storage Manager
ASME	American Society of Mechanical Engineers
ASN	Average Sample Number
ASP	Acceptance Sampling Plan
ASP	Acoustic Signal Processor
ASP	Attached Support Processor
ASP	Automated Spooling Priority
ASQC	American Society of Quality Control
ASR	Active Status Register
ASR	Address Shift Register
ASR	Amplitude Suppression Ratio
ASR	Analog Shift Register
ASR	Assigned Slot Release
ASR	Automatic Send-Receive
ASR	Available Supply Rate
ASS	Automatic Separation System
ASSM	Associative Memory
assoc	Association
asst	Assistant
AST	Accelerated Service Test
AST	Add-Subtract Time
AST	Automatic Scan Tracking
ASTM	American Society for Testing and Materials
ASTME	American Society of Tool and Manufacturing Engineers
async	Asynchronous
AT	Absolute Temperature
AT	Absolute Title
AT	Absolute Tolerance
AT	Accelerating Time
AT	Acceptance Testing
AT	Access Time
AT	Acetate Tape
AT	Acoustical Transitivity
AT	Activation Time
AT	Address Translator
AT	Ambient Temperature

AT	Anomalous Transmission
AT	Appropriate Technology
AT	Automatic Transmission
ATC	Air Traffic Control
ATC	Automated Technical Control
ATC	Automatic Tool Charger
ATDM	Asynchronous Time-Division Multiplexing
ATE	Automatic Test Equipment
ATI	Automatic Track Initiation
ATI	Average Total Inspection
ATL	Active Task List
ATM	Automatic Teller Machine
ATMS	Advanced Text Management System
atn	Attention
ATN	Augmented Transition Network
ATP	Alternative Term Plan
ATPG	Automatic Test Pattern Generation
ATR	Ambient Temperature Range
ATS	Active Tracking System
ATS	Administrative Terminal System
ATS	Analytic Trouble Shooting
ATS	Automated Test System
ATS	Automatic Transfer Service
ATT	American Telephone and Telegraph
ATT	Average Total Time
attr	Attribute
AU	Arithmetic Unit
AUT	Advanced User Terminal
aux	Auxiliary
AV	Absolute Value
AV	Acceleration Voltage
AV	Attribute Value
AV	Audio Visual
av	Audiovisual
av	Available
AVA	Absolute Virtual Address
AVC	Automatic Volume Control
AVD	Absolute Value Device
ave	Avenue
AVFD	Amplitude Versus Frequency Distortion
avg	Average
AVIP	Association of View-data Information Providers
AVR	Automatic Volume Recognition
AVS	Automatic Volume Sensing
AVT	Attribute Value Time
AW	Absorption Wavemeter
AWF	Acoustic Wave Filter
AWG	American Wire Gage
AWS	Active Work Space

BA	Bus Available
BAAS	British Association for the Advancement of Science
BAC	Bus Adapter Control
bal	Balance
BAL	Basic Assembly Language
BAM	Basic Access Method
BAM	Block Allocating Map
BAP	Basic Assembly Program
BAR	Base Address Register
BARSA	Billing, Account Receivable, Sales Analyses
BART	Bay Area Rapid Transit
BAS	Block Automation System
BAS	Business Accounting System
BASIC	Beginner's All-Purpose Symbolic Instruction Code
BAT	Best Available Technology
bat	Batch
BB	Begin Bracket
BBD	Bucket Brigade Devices
BBS	Business Batch System
BC	Bar Code
BC	Basic Control
BC	Binary Code
BC	Business Computer
BCB	Base Control Block
BCB	Bit Control Block
BCB	Buffer Control Block
BCC	Block Check Character
BCD	Binary Coded Decimal
BCD	Brightness Contrast Detail
BCH	Block Control Header
BCI	Basic Command Interpreter
BCL	Base-Coupled Logic
BCM	Bound Control Module
BCO	Binary Coded Octal
BCP	Byte Controlled Protocol
BCS	British Computer Society
BCU	Basic Counter Unit
BCU	Block Control Unit
bd	Board
BDAM	Basic Direct Access Method
BDE	Batch Data Exchange
BDES	Batch Data Exchange Services
BDM	Basic Data Management

BDP	Bulk Data Processing
BDP	Business Data Processing
BDU	Basic Device Unit
BE	Back End
BE	Bus Enable
BEM	Basic Editor Monitor
BEMA	Business Equipment Manufacturers Association
BER	Bit Error Rate
BERT	Bit Error Rate Test
BES	Basic Executive System
bet	Between
BETA	Business Equipment Trade Association
BEX	Broadband Exchange
BF	Blocking Factor
bf	Boldface
bg	Background
BI	Batch Input
BIC	Bureau of International Commerce
BIC	Byte Input Control
BIM	British Institute of Management
biog	Biography
biol	Biology
BIOS	Basic Input & Output Supervisor
BIS	Business Information System
BISAM	Basic Indexed Sequential Access Method
BIU	Basic Information Unit
BIU	Buffer Image Unit
BIU	Bus Interface Unit
bksp	Backspace
BL	Block Length
blk	Block
BLL	Below Lower Limit
BLM	Basic Language Machine
BLS	Bureau of Labor Statistics
BLU	Basic Link Unit
blvd	Boulevard
BM	Base Machine
BM	Basic Material
BM	Buffer Module
BM	Business Machine
BMC	Basic Monthly Charge
BMC	Block Multiplexer Channel
BMC	Bubble Memory Controller
BMC	Bulk Media Conversion
BMD	Bubble Memory Device
BML	Basic Machine Language
BMP	Batch Message Processing
BMS	Bit Mark Sequencing
BN	Block Number

BNN	Boundary Network Node
BO	Branch Office
BO	Byte Out
BOC	Basic Operating Company
BOE	Beginning Of Extent
BOF	Beginning Of File
BOM	Bill Of Materials
BOMP	Bill Of Material Processor
BOP	Basic Operator Panel
BOP	Bit-Oriented Protocol
BORAM	Block Oriented Random Access Memory
BOS	Basic Operating System
BOT	Beginning Of Tape
bot	Bottom
BP	Batch Processing
BPAM	Basic Partitioned Access Method
BPI	Bits Per Inch
BPI	Bytes Per Inch
BPL	Business Planning Language
BPM	Batch Processing Monitor
BPOS	Batch Processing Operating System
BPS	Basic Programming Support
BPS	Bits Per Second
BPS	Bytes Per Second
br	Break
BR	Break Request
bro	Brother
BS	Back Speed
BS	Backspace
BS	Brown and Sharp
BS	Business System
BSAM	Basic Sequential Access Method
BSC	Binary Synchronous Communication
BSCA	Binary Synchronous Communications Adapter
BSI	British Standards Institution
bskt	Basket
BSR	Basic Status Register
BSS	Bulk Storage System
bt	Between
BT	Burst Trapping
BTAM	Basic Telecommunications Access Method
BTC	Batch Terminal Controller
BTF	Bulk Transfer Facility
BTG	British Technology Group
BTL	Beginning Tape Label
BTM	Basic Transport Mechanism
BTP	Batch Transfer Program
BTR	Behind Tape Reader
BTS	Bound Task Set

BTU	**Basic Transmission Unit**
BTU	**British Thermal Unit**
BU	**Base Unit**
buf	**Buffer**
BUG	**Basic Update Generator**
bull	**Bulletin**
bur	**Bureau**
BUS	**Basic Utility System**
bus	**Business**
BWD	**Basic Work Data**

CA	Channel Adapter
CA	Communications Adapter
CA	Control Area
CAD	Computer Aided Design
CAD	Computer Assisted Drafting
CADAM	Computer Augmented Design And Manufacturing
CADD	Computer Aided Design and Drafting
CAE	Computer Assisted Engineering
CAI	Computer Analog Input
CAI	Computer Assisted Instruction
CAL	Common Assembly Language
CAL	Computer-Assisted Learning
CAL	Conversational Algebraic Language
calc	Calculate
CAM	Calculated Access Method
CAM	Communications Access Method
CAM	Content Addressable Memory
CAMP	Central Access Monitor Program
can	Cancel
cap	Capitalize
CAP	Computer Aided Programming
CAPC	Computer Aided Production Control
CAR	Channel Address Register
CAR	Check Authorization Record
CAR	Computer-Assisted Retrieval
carr	Carrier
CAS	Circuit And System
CAS	Computer Accounting System
CASA	Computer and Automated System Association
CASE	Computer-Aided Software Engineering
CASS	Coding Accuracy Support System
CASS	Common Address Space Section
cat	Catalog

CAT	Computer-Aided Testing
CAT	Computer-Aided Translation
CAT	Computerized Axial Topography
CATV	Community Antenna Television
CAU	Command Arithmetic Unit
CAW	Channel Address Word
CAX	Community Automatic Exchange
CAZ	Commutative Auto-Zero
CB	Citizen Band
CB	Communications Buffer
CBA	Cost Benefit Analyses
CBCT	Customer Bank Communications Terminal
CBI	Computer Based Instruction
CBMS	Computer-Based Message System
CC	Card Code
CC	Card Column
CC	Communications Computer
CC	Computer Center
CC	Condition Code
CC	Control Computer
CCA	Central Computer Agency
CCA	Common Communications Adapter
CCA	Communications Control Area
CCA	Current Cost Accounting
CCB	Character Control Block
CCB	Command Control Block
CCB	Configuration Control Board
CCB	Connection Control Block
CCCB	Completion Code Control Block
CCD	Charge Coupled Device
CCE	Channel Command Entry
CCF	Cobol Communications Facility
CCF	Controller Configuration Facility
CCH	Channel-Check Handler
CCHS	Cylinder-Cylinder Head Sector
CCIA	Computer and Communications Industries Association
CCM	Charge Coupled Memory
CCM	Communications Control Module
CCP	Character-Controlled Protocol
CCP	Communication Control Panel
CCP	Communications Control Program
CCPT	Controller Creation Parameter Table
CCR	Channel Control Routine
CCROS	Card Capacitor Read-Only Store
CCSA	Common Control Switching Arrangement
CCT	Carriage Control Tape
CCTV	Closed-Circuit Television
CCU	Central Control Unit
CCU	Channel Control Unit

CCU	Communications Control Unit
CCU	Computer Control Unit
CCW	Channel Command Word
cd	Card
CD	Chain Data
CD	Collision Detection
CD	Compact Disk
CD-ROM	Compact Disk - Read Only Memory
CDB	Corporate Data Base
CDC	Call Direction Code
CDC	Code Directing Character
CDC	Computer Display Channel
CDD	Common Data Dictionary
CDE	Contents Directory Entry
CDL	Computer Description Language
CDL	Computer Design Language
CDP	Certificate in Data Processing
CDP	Certified Data Processor
CDP	Communications Data Processor
CDRM	Cross-Domain Resource Manager
CDS	Central Dynamic System
CDS	Control Data Set
CDS	Control Display System
CDT	Command Definition Table
CDT	Communications Display Terminal
CDTL	Common Data Translation Language
CDU	Cartridge Disk Unit
CDV	Check Digit Verification
CE	Chip Enable
CE	Consumer Electronics
CE	Critical Examination
CE	Customer Engineering
CECUA	Conference of European Computer User Associations
CEI	Chip Enable Input
cent	Century
CEO	Comprehensive Electronic Office
CEP	Civil Engineering Package
cert	Certificate
CESD	Composite External Symbol Dictionary
CF	Carried Forward
CF	Count Forward
CFIA	Component Failure Impact Analysis
CFM	Cubic Feet per Minute
CFMS	Chained File Management System
CFP	Creation Facilities Program
CFS	Continuous Forms Stacker
CFS	Cubic Feet per Second
cg	Centigram
CG	Channel Grant

CG	Color Graphics
CG	Computer Graphics
CGMID	Character Generation Module Identifier
chap	Chapter
char	Character
CHAT	Cheep Access Terminal
CHCU	Channel Control Unit
CHI	Computer Human Interaction
CHIO	Channel Input/Output
CHIPS	Clearing House Interbank Payment System
chk	Check
chkpt	Checkpoint
chm	Chairman
CHPS	Character Per Second
chron	Chronology
CI	Communications Interface
CI	Configuration Item
CIA	Computer Industry Association
CIA	Computer Interface Adapter
CIB	Command Input Buffer
CIC	Communications Intelligence Channel
CICP	Communications Interrupt Control Program
CICS	Customer Information Control System
CID	Component Identification Number
CIDA	Channel Indirect Data Addressing
CIDF	Control Interval Definition Field
CIF	Central Information File
CIG	Computer Image Generation
CIL	Computer Interpreter Language
CIL	Condition-Incident Log
CIL	Core Image Library
CIM	Communications Interface Module
CIM	Computer Input Microfilm
CIM	Computer Integrated Manufacturing
CIOCS	Communication Input/Output Control System
CIPS	Canadian Information Processing Society
CIR	Current Instruction Register
circ	Circular
CIS	Central Information System
CIS	Control Indicator Set
CIS	Custom Integrated System
CIU	Central Interface Unit
CIU	Communication Interface Unit
CIU	Computer Interface Unit
CKD	Count Key Data
cl	Centiliter
CL	Command Language
CL	Control Line
CLA	Computer Law Association

CLA	Custom Logic Array
class	Classification
CLAT	Communication Line Adapter for Teletype
CLB	Central Logic Bus
CLC	Communications Line Control
CLC	Communications Link Controller
CLEAR	Closed Loop Evaluation And Reporting
CLI	Command Language Interpreter
CLIST	Command List
clk	Clock
CLP	Communication Line Processor
CLP	Current Line Pointer
CLS	Communications Line Switch
CLT	Communications Line Terminal
CLUE	Compiler Language Utility Extension
CLUT	Color Look-Up Table
cm	Centimeter
CM	Central Memory
CM	Communications Multiplexer
CM	Control Memory
CM	Control Module
CMA	Computer Management Association
CMA	Computer Monitor Adapter
CMB	Corrective Maintenance Burden
CMC	Communications Mag Card
CMC	Computer Numerical Control
CMC	Concurrent Media Conversion
cmd	Current
CMI	Computer Managed Instruction
CML	Common Mode Logic
CML	Current Mode Logic
CMM	Communications Multiplexed Module
CMOS	Complementary Metal Oxide Semiconductor
CMU	Control Maintenance Unit
CMS	Conversational Monitoring System
CN	Communications Network
CN	Contract Number
CN	Coordination Number
CNA	Communications Network Architecture
CNC	Communications Network Controller
CNC	Computerized Numerical Control
CNE	Communications Network Emulation
CNM	Communications Network Management
CNP	Communications Network Processor
cntl	Control
cntr	Counter
CO	Carry Out
CO	Console Output
COBOL	Common Business Oriented Language

COC	Computer On the Chip
COCS	Container Operating Control System
col	Column
COL	Computer Oriented Language
COLA	Cost Of Living Adjustment
coll	Collator
COM	Cassette Operating Monitor
COM	Computer Output Microfilm
COM	Computer Output Microform
COM	Computer Output Micrographics
comb	Combination
conc	Concentrated
cond	Condition
conf	Conference
cong	Congress
conj	Conjunction
const	Constant
contd	Continued
conv	Conversion
COP	Character-Oriented Protocol
COP	Communications Output Printer
corp	Corporation
corr	Correction
CORS	Canadian Operational Research Society
COS	Class Of Service
COS	Commercial Operating System
COSBA	Computer Services and Bureau Association
COT	Customer Oriented Terminal
CP	Card Punch
CP	Central Processor
CP	Command Processor
CP	Communication Processor
CP	Continuous Path
CP	Control Part
CP	Control Program
CP	Correspondence Printer
CPA	Certified Public Accountant
CPA	Channel Program Area
CPA	Critical Path Analysis
CPAB	Computer Programmer Aptitude Battery
CPB	Channel Program Block
CPC	Card Programmed Calculator
CPC	Computer process Control
CPE	Computer Performance Evaluation
CPE	Cross-Program Editor
CPF	Control Program Facility
CPH	Cost Per Hour
CPI	Changes Per Inch
CPI	Characters Per Inch

CPL	Characters Per Line
cpl	Complete
CPM	Cards Per Minute
CPM	Characters Per Minute
CPM	Critical Path Method
CPM	Cycles Per Minute
CPMA	Computer Peripheral Manufacturers Association
CPO	Concurrent Peripheral Operations
CPS	Card Programming System
CPS	Characters Per Second
CPS	Cycles Per Second
CPT	Chief Programmer Team
CPT	Customer Provided Terminal
CPU	Central Processing Unit
CR	Card Reader
CR	Carriage Return
CR	Carry Register
cr	Circle
CR	Command Register
CR	Communications Register
cr	Credit
CR	Critical Ratio
CRA	Catalogue Recovery Area
CRAM	Card Random Access Memory
CRBE	Conversational Remote Batch Entry
CRC	Cyclic Redundancy Check
CRCC	Cyclic Redundancy Check Character
CRE	Carrier Return Character
CRJE	Conversational Remote Job Entry
CROM	Control Read-Only Memory
CROS	Capacitor Read-Only Store
CRP	Channel Request Priority
CRT	Cathode Ray Tube
CRT	Computer Remote Terminal
crt	Critical
CRU	Card Reader Unit
CS	Chip Select
CS	Communication Services
CS	Communications System
CS	Computer Science
CS	Condition Subsequent
CS	Constructor Syntax
CS	Control Store
CSA	Canadian Standards Association
CSA	Computer Services Association
CSB	Communication Scanner Base
CSC	Computer Society of Canada
CSMP	Continuous System Modeling Program
CSN	Computer Service Network

CSO	Computer Service Office
CSP	Communications Symbiont Processor
CSR	Console Send-Receive
CST	Channel Status Message
CSU	Customer Service Unit
CSU	Customer Set Up
CSW	Channel Status Word
CT	Cable Transfer
CT	Cassette Tape
CT	Change Ticker
CT	Communications Terminal
CTB	Concentrator Terminal Buffer
CTCA	Channel-To-Channel Adapter
ctr	Center
CTS	Carriage Tape Simulator
CTS	Clear To Send
CTS	Conversational Terminal System
CTV	Cable Television
CU	Control Unit
CU	Correlation Unit
cu	Cubic
CU	Customer Use
CUA	Computer Users Association
CUDN	Common User Data Network
CUE	Computer Utilization Efficiency
CUE	Configuration Utilization Evaluator
CUG	Closed User Group
cum	Cumulative
CUTS	Computer Users Tape System
CVD	Chemical Vapor Deposition
cw	Clockwise
CW	Command Word
CW	Continuous Wave
CW	Control Word
CWP	Communicating Word Processor
CWP	Computer Word Processing
cy	Carry
cy	Currency
cy	Cycle
cyl	Cylinder

DA	Data Administrator
DA	Data Available
da	Deka

DA	Demand Assignment
DA	Design Automation
DA	Destination Address
DA	Device Adapter
DA	Differential Analyzer
DA	Digital-to-Analog
DA	Direct Access
DA	Direct Action
DA	Directory Assistance
DA	Disk Action
DA	Display Adapter
DAA	Direct Access Arrangement
DAC	Data Accepted
DAC	Data Acquisition and Control
DAC	Design Augmented by Computer
DAC	Digital-to-Analog Computer
DAC	Digital-to-Analog Converter
DADS	Data Acquisition and Display System
DAF	Destination Address Field
DAI	Direct Access Information
DAL	Data Access Language
DAL	Digital Access Line
DAM	Data Addressed Memory
DAM	Direct Access Method
DAMA	Demand-Assigned Multiple-Access
DAP	Data Access Protocol
DAPS	Direct Access programming System
DAR	Damage Assessment Routine
DAS	Data Access Security
DAS	Data Acquisition System
DAS	Data Analysis System
DAS	Data Automation System
DASD	Direct Access Storage Device
DAT	Digital Audio Tape
DAT	Disk Allocation Table
DAT	Dynamic Address Translation
DAV	Data Above Voice
DB	Data Bank
DB	Data Base
DB	Data Bus
db	Decibel
DBA	Data Base Administrator
DBC	Data Base Computer
DBCB	Device Base Control Block
DBD	Data Base Description
DBDA	Data Base Design Aid
DBDL	Data Base Definition Language
DBE	Data Bus Enable
DBF	Data Base Facility

dbl	Double
DBMS	Data Base Management Software
DBMS	Data Base Management System
DBS	Direct Broadcast Satellite
DBTG	Data Base Task Group
DC	Data Cartridge
DC	Data Cassette
DC	Data Center
DC	Data Channel
DC	Data Classifier
DC	Data Code
DC	Data Communication
DC	Data Conversion
DC	Data Counter
DC	Decimal Classification
DC	Device Control
DC	Device Controller
DC	Digital Computer
DC	Direct Control
DC	Direct Current
DC	Disk Controller
DC	Double Column
DCA	Distributed Communications Architecture
DCB	Data Control Block
DCB	Device Control Block
DCC	Digital Communications Console
DCD	Data Carrier Detect
DCE	Data Circuit Equipment
DCE	Digital Communications Equipment
DCF	Data Count Field
DCF	Digital Communications Facility
DCH	Data Channel
DCI	Direct Channel Interface
DCL	Data Control List
DCS	Data Collection System
DCS	Data Communications Subsystem
DCS	Defense Communications System
DCS	Distributed Computer System
DCT	Device Characteristics Table
DCT	Dispatcher Control Table
DCTL	Direct-Coupled Transistor Logic
DCU	Data Control Unit
DCU	Display Control Unit
DCW	Data Control Work
DD	Dark Detail
DD	Data Definition
DD	Data Dictionary
DD	Data Directory
DD	Data Division

DD	Diffused Device
DD	Digital Data
DD	Digital Device
DD	Direct Drive
DD	Double Deck
DDA	Demand Deposit Accounting
DDA	Digital Differential Analyzer
DDA	Direct Disk Attachment
DDB	Device Descriptor Block
DDC	Direct Digital Control
DDCMP	Digital Data Communications Message Protocol
DDD	Direct Distance Dialing
DDDL	Dictionary Data Definition Language
DDG	Digital Display Generator
DDL	Data Definition Language
DDL	Data Description Language
DDM	Device Descriptor Module
DDN	Defense Data Network
DDP	Data-gram Delivery Protocol
DDP	Distributed Data Processing
DDR	Dynamic Device Reconfiguration
DDS	Data Distribution System
DDS	Data-phone Digital Service
DDS	Digital Data System
DDS	Dynamic Dispatch System
DDSA	Digital Data Service Adapter
DDT	Data Description Table
DDU	Disk Drive Unit
DE	Data Entry
DE	Dictating Equipment
DEA	Data Encryption Algorithm
DEB	Data Extend Block
DECUS	Digital Equipment Computer Users Society
DEDB	Data Entry Data Base
def	Definition
DEF	Destination Element Field
deg	Degree
DEL	Direct Exchange Line
dem	Demand
denom	Denomination
dept	Department
DES	Data Encryption Standard
DEU	Data Encryption Unit
DF	Data Field
DF	Destination Field
DF	Device Flag
DFC	Data Flow Control
DFC	Disk File Controller
DFT	Diagnostic Function Test

DFT	Discrete Fourier Translator
DFU	Data File Utility
DG	Data General
dh	Deadhead
DH	Design Handbook
DHCF	Distributed Host Command Facility
DI	Device Independence
DI	Digital Input
DI	Digital Integrator
DI	Discrete Input
DIAL	Data Interchange Application Level
diam	Diameter
DIB	Data Integrity Block
DIC	Data Interchange Code
dict	Dictionary
DID	Digital Information Display
DID	Direct Inward Dialing
DIF	Device Input Format
dig	Digital
DIL	Dual-In-Line
DINA	Distributed Information for Network Architecture
DIOCB	Device Input/Output Control Block
dir	Director
dist	District
DIV	Data In Voice
div	Division
DIVA	Data Input Voice Answer-back
DL	Data Language
DL	Data Link
DL	Data List
DLA	Data Link Adapter
DLAT	Directory Look-Aside Table
DLC	Data Link Control
DLE	Data Link Escape
DLM	Digital Logic Module
DLT	Data Loop Transceiver
DLU	Data Line Unit
DM	Data Management
DM	Design Manual
DM	Directional Microphone
DMA	Direct Memory Access
DMA	Drum Memory Assembly
DMAC	Direct Memory Access Channel
DMF	Disc Management Facility
DMH	Device Message Handler
DML	Data Manipulation Language
DML	Device Media Language
DMO	Data Management Officer
DMS	Data Management System

DMU	Data Management Unit
DMY	Day-Month-Year
DN	Data Name
DNA	Digital Network Architecture
DNA	Distributed Network Architecture
DNC	Direct Numerical Control
DNIC	Data Network Identification Code
DNL	Do Not Load
DNL	Dynamic Noise Limiter
DO	Digital Output
DOC	Direct Operating Costs
doc	Document
DOD	Direct Outward Dialing
DOF	Device Output Format
DOI	Department Of Industry
dol	Dollar
DOP	Developing Out Paper
DOR	Digital Optical Recording
DOS	Disk Operating System
DOSF	Distributed Office Support Facility
doz	Dozen
DP	Data Processing
DP	Distribution Point
DP	Double Precision
DP	Draft Printer
DP	Dynamic Programming
DPA	Display Printer Adapter
DPB	Dynamic Pool Block
DPC	Data Processing Center
DPC	Disc Pack Controller
DPCX	Distributed Processing Control Executive
DPDT	Double-Pole Double-Throw
DPH	Disc Pack Handler
DPM	Data Plant Management
DPM	Data Processing Machine
DPM	Data Processing Manager
DPM	Distributed Presentation Management
DPM	Documents Per Minute
DPMA	Data Processing Management Association
DPS	Data Processing System
DPS	Disc Programming System
DPS	Distributed Presentation Services
DPS	Document Processing System
DPSA	Data Processing Supplies Association
DPSK	Differential Phase Shift Keying
DPU	Display Processor Unit
DQCB	Disc Queue Control Block
DR	Data Report
dr	Doctor

DRAM	Dynamic Random Access Memory
DRAW	Digital Read After Write
DRC	Data Recording Control
DRCS	Dynamically Re-definable Character Set
DRD	Data Recording Device
DRDS	Dynamic Reconfiguration Data Set
DREAM	Design Realization Evaluation And Modeling
DRO	Destructive Read-Out
DRO	Digital Read-Out
DRQ	Data Ready Queue
DRT	Data Terminal Ready
DS	Data Set
DS	Data Structure
DS	Direct Scanning
DS	Directivity Signal
DSAC	Data Set Authors Credential
DSAF	Destination Sub-Area Field
DSC	Disc Storage Controller
DSCA	Default System Control Area
DSCB	Data Set Control Block
DSCP	Data Services Command Processor
DSD	Data Set Definition
DSDD	Double Sided Double Density
DSDT	Data Set Definition Table
DSE	Data Set Extension
DSE	Data Switching Exchange
DSE	Distributed Systems Environment
DSI	Data Stream Interface
DSI	Digital Signal Interpolation
DSI	Digital Speech Interpolation
dsk	Disk
DSL	Data Set Label
DSL	Development Support Library
DSLO	Distributed System License Option
DSM	Data Services Manager
DSN	Distributed Systems Network
DSO	Data Set Optimizer
DSO	Direct System Output
DSP	Digital Signal Processor
dspl	Display
DSQD	Double Sided Quad Density
DSR	Data Set Ready
DSRB	Data Services Request Block
DSS	Digital Subset
DSS	Disc Storage Subsystem
DSS	Dynamic Support System
DST	Data Services Task
DST	Device Service Task
DSU	Data Service Unit

DSU	Digital Service Unit
DSU	Disk Storage Unit
DSW	Device Status Word
DSX	Distributed System Executive
DT	Data Table
DT	Data Terminal
DT	Data Transmission
DT	Dial Tone
DT	Display Terminal
DTC	Data Transmission Channel
DTC	Desk Top Computer
DTD	Digital Television Display
DTE	Data Terminal Equipment
DTF	Define The File
DTL	Diode-Transistor Logic
DTMF	Dual-Tone Multi-Frequency
DTMS	Data Base and Transaction Management System
DTPA	Dynamic Transient Pool Area
DTPM	Dynamic Transient Pool Management
DTR	Distribution Tape Reel
DTS	Data Transfer Sequence
DTSRS	Dynamic Transient Segment Register Save
DTT	Domain Tip Technology
DTU	Display Terminal Unit
DU	Display Unit
DUP	Disk Utility Program
dup	Duplicate
DUT	Device Under Test
DUV	Data Under Voice
DV	Dependent Variable
DVMS	Digital Voice Messaging System
DVST	Direct View Storage Tube
DVT	Device Vector Table
DW	Daisy Wheel
DXC	Data Exchange Control
DXS	Data Exchange System

ea	Each
EA	Effective Address
EA	Element Activity
EA	Energy Analysis
EA	Environment Analysis
EAD	Equipment Allowance Document
EAE	Extended Arithmetic Element

EAM	Electrical Accounting Machine
EAN	European Article Number
EAP	Emulator Application Program
EAR	Extended Address Register
EARL	Easy Access Report Language
EAU	Extended Arithmetic Unit
EAX	Electronic Automatic Exchange
EB	Electronic Beam
EB	Event Block
EBAM	Electron Beam Accessed Memory
EBC	Electronic Business Communications
EBR	Electron Beam Recorder
ec	Economics
EC	Electromagnetic Communications
EC	Electromagnetic Compatibility
EC	Electronic Charge
EC	Electronic Computer
EC	Electronic Contact
EC	Engineering Change
EC	Extended Control
ECB	Event Control Block
ECC	Error Checking and Correction
ECC	Error Correction Code
ECCCS	Emergency Command Control Communications System
ECD	Estimated Completion Date
ECIP	European Cooperation in Information Processing
ECM	Extended Core Memory
ECMA	European Computer Manufacturers Association
ECO	Engineering Change Order
ECOM	Electronic Computer Originated Mail
ECR	Electronic Cash Register
ECS	Expanded Character Set
ECSA	European Computing Services Association
ECT	Environment Control Table
ECU	Electronic Control Unit
ed	Editor
EDC	Electronic Digital Computer
EDC	Error Detection and Correction
EDC	Estimated Date of Completion
EDC	Extended Device Control
EDD	Electronic Document Distribution
EDI	Electronic Data Interchange
EDL	Electromagnetic Delay Line
EDL	Emulation Design Language
EDOS	Extended Disc Operating System
EDP	Electronic Data Processing
EDPE	Electronic Data Processing Equipment
EDPM	Electronic Data Processing Machine
EDPS	Electronic Data Processing System

EDS	Electronic Data Switching
EDS	Electronic Data System
EDS	Engineering Data System
EDS	Engineering Design System
EDS	Exchangeable Disk Store
EDSAC	Electronic Delay Storage Automatic Computer
EDST	Elastic Diaphragm Switch Technology
edt	Editor
EDT	Engineering Design Text
educ	Education
EE	Electrical Engineer
EE	Errors Accepted
EEI	Essential Elements of Information
EEP	Electronic Evaluation and Procurement
EEP	Electronic Event Programmer
EEROM	Electrically Erasable Read-Only Memory
EF	Execution Function
EF	Extended Facility
EF	External Flag
EFL	Error Frequency Limit
EFOP	Expanded Function Operator Panel
EFS	External Function Store
EFT	Electronic Funds Transfer
EFTS	Electronic Funds Transfer System
eg	For Example (Exempli gratia)
EHF	Extremely High Frequency
EI	Enable Interrupt
EI	Error Indicator
EIA	Electronics Industries Association
EIC	Equipment Identification Code
EIII	European Independent Informatics Industry
EIN	European Informatics Network
EIOS	Extended Input Output System
EIPC	European Institute of Printed Circuits
EIRV	Error Interrupt Request Vector
EIS	Environmental Impact Statement
EIS	Extended Instruction Set
EJCC	Eastern Joint Computer Conference
EL	End of Line
EL	External Link
ELA	Extender Line Adapter
elec	Electric
elem	Elementary
ELF	Extremely-Low-Frequency
ELM	Error Log Manager
elt	Element
EM	Electronic Mail
EM	Extended Memory
EMC	End of Medium Character

EMH	Expedited Message Handling
EMI	Electro-Magnetic Interface
EMP	Electro-Magnetic Pulse
EMS	Electronic Message Service
enbl	Enable
enc	Enclosure
encyc	Encyclopedia
eng	English
ENS	Extended Network Service
env	Envelope
EO	Enable Output
EO	Engineering Order
EOA	End Of Address
EOB	End Of Block
EOC	End Of Card
EOC	End Of Chain
EOD	End Of Data
EOE	End Of Extend
EOF	End Of File
EOF	End Of Form
EOI	End Of Inquiry
EOI	End Of Item
EOJ	End Of Job
EOL	End Of Line
EOL	End Of List
EOM	End Of Message
EOP	End Of Program
EOQ	Economic Order Quantity
EOR	End Of Record
EOR	End Of Reel
EOR	End Of Report
EOR	End Of Run
EOS	Extended Operating System
EOT	End Of Tape
EOT	End Of Text
EOT	End Of Transmission
EOV	End Of Volume
EP	Emulator Program
EPA	Environmental Protection Agency
EPL	European Program Library
EPO	Emergency Power-Off
EPR	Error Pattern Register
EPROM	Erasable Programmable Read Only Memory
EPSS	Experimental Packet Switched Service
EPST	Extended Partition Specification Table
eql	Equal
eqpt	Equipment
ER	Established Reliability
ER	Explicit Route

ER	Exponent Register
ERA	Electronic Representatives Association
ERB	Execution Request Block
ERC	Error Entry Count
EREP	Environmental Recording Editing and Printing
ERM	Error Recovery Manager
ERMA	Electronic Recording Method of Accounting
ERP	Error Recovery Procedures
err	Error
ERU	External Run Unit
ES	Expert System
ES	External Store
ESB	Electrical Standards Board
esc	Escape
ESC	Escape Character
ESD	External Symbol Dictionary
ESL	European System Language
ESN	Effective Segment Number
ESN	External Segment Name
esp	Especially
ESR	Equivalent Series Resistance
ESS	Electronic Switching System
est	Estimated
ESTV	Error Statistics by Tape Volume
ESV	Error Statistics by Volume
ET	Eastern Time
ET	Emerging Technology
ET	End of Text
ETB	End of transmission Block
etc	Etcetera
ETC	Extended Text Compositor
ETOS	Extended Tape Operating System
ETP	Electrical Tough Pitch
ETP	Extended Tape Processing
ETP	Extended Term Plan
ETS	Electronic Test System
EU	End-User
EU	Execution Unit
EUF	End User Facility
EV	End Vector
EVA	Error Volume Analysis
evid	Evidence
EVIL	Extensible Video Interactive Language
EVM	Extended Virtual Machine
EVR	Electronic Video Recording
ex	Example
exc	Except
exec	Executive
exp	Exponent

exp	Express
exp	Expression
EXR	Exception Request
ext	Extension

FA	Facilitating Agency
FA	Factory Automation
FA	Field Address
FA	Final Address
fac	Factual
FAC	File Access Channel
FAC	Function Authority Credential
FACE	Field Alterable Control Element
FACT	Fully Automatic Compiling Technique
FADP	Federal Automatic Data Processing
FAL	File Access Listener
FAMS	Forecasting And Modeling System
FAP	Failure Analysis Program
FAPS	Financial Analysis and Planning System
FAR	File Address Register
FASB	Financial Accounting Standards Board
FAST	Fast Access Storage Technology
FAST	File Analysis and Selection Technique
FATS	Fast Analysis of Tape Surfaces
fax	Facsimile
FB	File Block
FB	Fixed Block
FBA	Fixed Block Architecture
FBT	Facility Block Table
FC	Flow Controller
FC	Flux Change
FC	Font Change
FC	Function Code
FCB	File Control Block
FCB	Forms Control Buffer
FCB	Function Control Block
FCC	Federal Communications Commission
FCC	Font Change Character
FCCTS	Federal Cobol Compiler Testing Service
FCI	Flux Changing per Inch
FCL	Format Control Language
FCO	Field Change Order
FCP	File Control Processor
FCP	File Control Program

FCS	Fixed Control Storage
FCS	Frame Check Sequence
FCU	File Control Unit
FD	File Definition
FD	File Description
FD	Floppy Disk
FD	Full Duplex
FDC	Floppy Disk Controller
FDD	Flexible Disk Drive
FDD	Floppy Disk Drive
FDL	Forms Description Language
FDM	Frequency Division Multiplexing
FDMA	Frequency Division Multiple-Access
FDP	Form Description Program
FDR	Fast Dump Restore
FDR	File Data Register
FDS	Flexible Disk System
FDT	Function Data Table
FDU	Form Description Utility
FE	Field Engineering
FE	Format Effector
FE	Front End
FEA	Finite Element Analysis
FEC	Forward Error Correction
FECB	File Extend Control Block
FECP	Front End Communications Processor
fed	Federal
FEFO	First Ended First Out
feg	Figurative
FEP	Front-End Processor
FES	Forms Entry System
FET	Field Effect Transistor
FF	Fast Forward
FF	Field Frequency
FF	Flip Flop
FF	Form Feed
FFA	Function to Function Architecture
FFN	Full Function Node
FFS	Formatted File System
fg	Foreground
FH	Field Handler
FH	File Handler
FH	Fixed Head
FHD	Fixed Head Disk
FHF	Fixed Head File
FHP	Fixed Header Prefix
FI	Format Identifier
FIB	File Information Block
FIC	First In Chain

FICB	File Identification Control Block
FID	Format Identification
FIF	Family Information Facility
FIFF	First In First Fit
FIFO	First In First Out
fin	Finance
FIP	Finance Image Processor
FIPS	Federal Information Processing Standards
FIR	File Indirect Register
FIR	Finite Impulse Response
FIT	File Inquiry Technique
FJCC	Fall Joint Computer Conference
FKA	Formerly Known As
fld	Field
FL	Field Length
FLOPS	Floating Point Operations Per Second
FM	Facilities Management
FM	File Management
FM	File Manager
FM	Format Manager
FM	Frequency Modulation
FMD	Function Management Data
FMH	Function Management Header
FML	File Manipulation Language
FMS	File Management Supervisor
FMS	Flexible Manufacturing System
fn	Footnote
FN	Functional Network
FNR	File Next Register
FNS	Feedback Node Set
FOD	Function Operational Design
fol	Folio
FOL	Function Of Lines
for	Foreign
FOS	Function Operational Specification
FP	File Processor
FP	Floating Point
FP	Frame Pointer
FP	Function Processor
FPH	Floating Point Hardware
FPL	File Parameter List
FPLA	Field Programmable Logic Array
FPM	Feet Per Minute
FPP	Floating Point Processor
FPR	Floating Point Register
FPROM	Field Programmable Read-Only Memory
FPS	Feet Per Second
FPS	Financial Planning System
FPT	File Parameter Table

FPU	File Processing Unit
FPU	Floating Point Unit
FR	File Register
FR	Final Report
FR	Final Request
fr	French
fract	Fraction
FRD	Functional Requirements Document
freq	Frequency
FRL	Frame Representation Language
FROM	Fusible Read-Only Memory
FRR	Functional Recovery Routine
frt	Freight
FRU	Field Replaceable Unit
frwy	Freeway
FS	Field Separator
FS	Field Service
FS	File Separator
FS	Full Scale
FS	Function Select
FS	Future Series
FSA	Field Search Argument
FSCB	File System Control Block
FSE	Full Screen Editor
FSK	Frequency Shift Keying
FSN	File Sequence Number
FSP	Full Screen Processing
FSR	Full-Scale Range
FSS	Federal Supply Schedule
FST	File Status Table
FT	Format Type
FT	Frequency and Time
ft	Foot
FTA	Fault Tree Analysis
FTE	Frame Table Entry
FTLP	Fixed Term Lease Plan
FTI	Fixed Time Interval
FTP	File Transfer Protocol
FTP	Fixed Term Plan
FTS	Federal Telecommunication System
FU	Field Unit
FU	Functional Unit
fut	Future
FW	First Word
FWA	First Word Address
fwd	Forward
FY	Fiscal Year
FYI	For Your Information
FYIG	For Your Information and Guidance

GA	General Average
GA	Global Address
GA	Graphic Adapter
gal	Gallon
GAM	Graphic Access Method
GAO	General Accounting Office
GAP	General Accounting Package
GAP	Graphics Application Program
GB	General Business
gb	Gigabyte
GBS	General Business System
GCR	Group Coded Recording
GD	Global Data
GD	Graphics Display
GD	Group Delay
GDG	Generation Data Group
gen	General
gent	Gentlemen
ger	German
GERT	Graphical Evaluation and Review Technique
GFI	Group Fault Interrupter
GI	Ground Insulation
GIGO	Garbage In Garbage Out
GIS	Generalized Information system
GJP	Graphic Job Processor
gloss	Glossary
gm	Gram
GM	Graphic Machine
GM	Group Mark
GN	Ground Noise
gnd	Ground
GNR	Guest Name Record
GO	General Operations
GO	General Order
GO	Generated Output
govt	Government
GP	General Purpose
GP	Grace Periods
GP	Graphic Package
GP	Graphic Processor
gp	Group
GPC	General Peripheral Controller
GPC	General Purpose Computer

GPI	Ground Position Indicator
GPIA	General Purpose Interface Adapter
GPIB	General Purpose Interface Bus
GPNNC	General Purpose Non-Numerical Computer
GPS	General Problem Storage
GPS	Graphic Programming Services
GPSS	General Purpose Simulation System
GPT	General Purpose Terminal
GPU	Graphic Processing Unit
GR	General Records
GR	General Register
GR	Ground Relay
gr	Greek
GRF	Geographic Reference File
GRS	General Records Schedule
GRS	General Register Stack
GRS	General Reporting System
GS	Graphics System
GS	Group Separator
GSAM	Generalized Sequential Access Method
GSE	Ground Support Equipment
GSP	Graphic Subroutine Package
GSR	Global Share Resources
GT	Graphics Terminal
GT	Greater Than
gtd	Guaranteed
GTF	General Trace Facility
GTF	Generalized Trace Facility
GTP	Graphic Transform Package

HA	Hazard Analysis
HAM	High Availability Manager
hand	Handling
hb	Handbook
HCF	Host Command Facility
HCP	Host Command Processor
HCP	Host Communication Processor
HCT	Hard Copy Task
HD	Hierarchical Direction
HD	High Density
HDA	Head Disc Assembly
HDAM	Hierarchical Direct Access Method
hdqrs	Headquarters
hdr	Header

HER	Human Error Rate
HF	High Frequency
HHC	Hand Held Computer
HIC	Hybrid Integrated Circuit
HIDAM	Hierarchical Indexed Direct Access Method
HIDM	High Information Delta Modulation
HIM	Hardware Interface Module
HIP	Host Interface Processor
hir	Hierarchy
HIS	Homogeneous Information Sets
HISAM	Hierarchical Indexed Sequential Access Method
HIT	High Isolation Transformer
HL	High Level
HLI	Host Language Interface
HLL	High Level Language
HMI	Hardware Monitor Interface
HNA	Hierarchical Network Architecture
HNR	Handwritten Numeral Recognition
HOF	Head Of Form
HOL	High Order Language
hor	Horizontal
hp	Horsepower
HPF	Highest Probable Frequency
hr	Hour
HS	Hierarchical Sequential
HS	High Speed
HSAM	Hierarchical Sequential Access Method
HSM	High Speed Memory
HSP	High Speed Printer
HSR	High Speed Reader
ht	Height
HTC	Horizontal Tabulation Character
HTL	High Threshold Logic
HV	High Voltage
hw	Hardware
hz	Hertz

IA	Integrated Adapter
IAC	Interactive Array Computer
IAL	International Algebraic Language
IAP	Industry Applications Programs
IAR	Instruction Address Register
IAS	Interactive Application System
IBI	Intergovernmental Bureau for Informatics

ibid	Ibidem
IBM	International Business Machines
IBN	Indexed By Name
IBRO	Inter-Bank Computer Bureau
IBT	Interrupt Bit Table
IC	Instruction Counter
IC	Integrated Circuit
ICA	International Communication Association
ICA	Integrated Communications Adapter
ICAM	Integrated Communications Access Method
ICAMP	Integrated Computer Aided Manufacturing Program
ICB	Interrupt Control Bloc
ICC	Integrated Communications Controller
ICC	Inter-Computer Coupler
ICC	International Computer Center
ICCE	International Council for Computers in Education
ICCF	Interactive Computing and Control Facility
ICCP	Institute for Certification of Computer Professionals
ICDS	Input Command Data Set
ICE	In-Circuit Emulation
ICG	Interactive Computer Graphics
ICR	Independent Component Release
ICS	Institute of Computer Science
ICS	Interactive Counting System
ICST	Institute for Computer Sciences and Technology
ICV	Initial Chaining Value
ICW	Interrupted Continuous Wave
id	Idem
id	Identifier
IDA	Integrated Disk Adapter
IDCB	Immediate Device Control Block
IDF	Internal Distribution Frame
idl	Idle
IDM	Intelligent Database Machine
IDMS	Integrated Database Management System
IDN	Integrated Digital Network
IDP	Institute of Data Processing
IDP	Integrated Data Processing
IDPM	Institute of Data Processing Management
IDS	Integrated Data Store
IDSTN	Integrated Digital Switching and Transmission Network
IDT	Intelligent Data Terminal
IEC	Integrated Electronic Component
IEEE	Institute of Electrical and Electronics Engineers
IEO	Integrated Electronic Office
IERE	Institution of Electronic and Radio Engineers
IF	Intermediate Frequency
IFA	Integrated File Adapter
IFAC	International Federation of Automatic Control

IFB	Invitation For Bid
IFCB	Interrupt Fan Control Block
IFIP	International Federation of Information Processing
IFP	Integrated File Processor
IGES	Initial Graphic Exchange Standard
IGFET	Insulated Gate Field Effect Transistor
IHF	Institute of High Fidelity
IIA	Institute of Internal Auditors
ILBT	Interrupt Level Branch Table
IM	Intelligent Modularity
IMC	Institute of Measurement and Control
IMI	Intermediate Machine Instruction
IMIS	Integrated Management Information System
IMP	Interface Message Processor
impe	Imperative
IMR	Interruption Mark Register
IMS	Information Management System
IMSI	Information Management System Interface
IMV	Instruction Memory Unit
IMX	Inquiry Message Exchange
in	Inch
in	Increase
IN	Index Number
IN	Information Network
inc	Incorporated
incl	Including
incr	Increment
ind	Index
ind	Indicator
info	Information
init	Initialize
inj	Injunction
inp	Input
INP	Intelligent Network Processor
inst	Instant
inst	Institute
inst	Instrument
int	Internal
inten	Intensity
interp	Interpreter
intl	International
intr	Interrupt
inv	Invoice
IO	Input Output
IOAU	Input Output Access Unit
IOB	Input Output Block
IOC	Initial Operational Capacity
IOC	Input Output Controller
IOCR	Input Output Control Routine

IOCS	Input Output Control System
IOM	Input Output Multiplex
IOP	Input Output Processor
IOQ	Input Output Queue
IOS	Input Output Supervisor
IP	Information Processing
IP	Information Provider
IPA	Information Processing Architecture
IPC	Illustrated Parts Catalog
IPC	Industrial Process Control
IPC	Integrated Peripheral Channel
IPCS	Interactive Problem Control System
IPE	Institution of Production Engineers
IPL	Information Processing Language
IPL	Initial Program Load
IPL	Initial Program Loader
IPL	Initial Program Loading
IPM	Inches Per Minute
IPO	Installation Productivity Option
IPR	Isolated Pacing Response
IPS	Inches Per Second
IPS	Information Processing System
IPS	Installation Performance Specification
IPSS	International Packet Switched Service
IPT	Improved Programming Technologies
IQF	Interactive Query Facility
IQL	Incoming Quality Level
IR	Index Register
IR	Indicator Register
IR	Industrial Relations
IR	Industrial Robot
IR	Information Retrieval
IR	Instruction Register
IR	Interrupt Request
IRA	Individual Retirement Account
IRBT	Intelligent Remote Batch Terminal
IRC	Information Retrieval Center
IRC	International Record Carrier
IRE	Institute of Radio Engineers
IRIS	Instantaneous Retrieval Information System
IRL	Information Retrieval Language
IRM	Information Resource Management
IRMS	Information Retrieval Management System
IRR	Internal Rate of Return
irreg	Irregular
IRS	Information Retrieval Service
IRS	Inquiry and Reporting System
IRS	Internal Revenue Service
IRSS	Intelligent Remote Station Support

IS	Information Separator
ISAM	Index Sequential Access Method
ISC	Integrated Storage Control
ISDN	Integrated Services Digital Network
ISE	Institute for Software Engineering
ISI	Intelligent Standard Interface
ISL	Initial System Load
ISL	Integrated Schottky Logic
ISO	Independent Sales Organization
ISO	International Standards Organization
ISR	Information Storage and Retrieval
ISR	Input Select and Reset
ISSCC	International Solid State Circuits Conference
IST	Input Stack Tape
IST	Interrupt Service Task
IT	Information Technology
IT	Input Terminal
IT	Intelligent Terminal
it	Interface
ital	Italics
ITB	Intermediate Text Block
ITC	Indent Tab Character
ITC	Investment Tax Credit
ITF	Interactive Terminal Facility
itin	Itinerary
ITR	Isolation Test Routine
ITS	Invitation To Send
ITU	International Telecommunication Union
IU	Information Unit
IU	Input Unit
IUP	Installed User Procedure
IVD	Ion Vapor Deposition
IVP	Installation Verification Procedure
IWP	International Word Processing

JA	Job Analysis
JB	Junction Box
JC	Joint Communications
JCB	Job Control Block
JCC	Job Control Card
JCFI	Job Control File Internal
JCFS	Job Control File Source
JCIT	Jerusalem Conference on Information Technology
JCL	Job Control Language

JCP	Job Control Program
JCS	Job Control Statement
JECS	Job Entry Central Services
JEDEC	Joint Electron Device Engineering Council
JEPS	Job Entry Peripheral Services
JES	Job Entry Subsystem
JES	Job Entry System
JET	Journal Entries Transfer
JFET	Junction Field-Effect Transistor
JIS	Job Information Station
JJL	Josephson Junction Logic
JL	Job Library
JM	Job Memory
JOC	Job Order Costing
JOD	Journal Of Development
JP	Job Processor
JPA	Job Pack Area
JR	Job Rotation
JR	Joint Return
JS	Job Services
JS	Job Set
JS	Job Statement
JSL	Job Specification Language
JT	Job Table
JUG	Joint Users Group

ka	Kiloampere
kb	Kilobyte
kbd	Keyboard
kc	Kilocycle
KCU	Keyboard Control Unit
KD	Key Definition
KDE	Keyboard Data Entry
KDS	Key Display System
KF	Key File
kg	Kilogram
KGM	Key Generator Module
kh	Kilohour
KIM	Keyboard Input Matrix
KIPS	Knowledge Information Processing System
KIS	Keep It Short
KIS	Keep It Simple
KIS	Keyboard Input Simulation
KL	Key Length

km	Kilometer
KOPS	Thousands of Operations Per Seconds
KR	Key Register
KRL	Knowledge Representation Language
KSH	Key Strokes per Hour
KSR	Keyboard Send Receive
KT	Key Tape
KTM	Key Transport Module
KTR	Keyboard Typing Re-perforator
kw	Kilowatt
KWIC	Key-Word In Context
KWOC	Key-Word Out of Context

LA	Line Adapter
LA	Line Art
LA	Local Address
LA	Logical Address
LA	Logical Area
lab	Laboratory
LADT	Local Area Data Transport
LAN	Local Area Network
lang	Language
LAP	Link Access Procedure
LAP	Link Access Protocol
LAPB	Link Access Protocol Balanced
LAS	Local Address Space
LASAR	Logic Automated Stimulus And Response
LASP	Local Attached Support Processor
lat	Latitude
LATA	Local Address and Transport Areas
LAU	Line Adapter Unit
LB	Line Buffer
LB	Logical Block
lb	Pound
LBG	Load Balancing Group
lbl	Label
LBN	Logical Block Number
LBR	Laser Beam Recording
LBT	Listen Before Talk
LC	Line Concentrator
LC	Line Control
LC	Logic Circuit
LC	Logical Choice
LC	Logical Comparison

LC	Loop Circuit
LC	Loudness Control
LC	Low Cost
LC	Lower Case
LCB	Line Control Block
LCB	Link Control Block
LCC	Ledger Card Computer
LCC	Life Cycle Costs
LCD	Liquid Crystal Display
LCDDS	Leased Circuit Digital Data Service
LCL	Lower Control Limit
LCN	Local Computer Network
LCP	Language Conversion Program
LCP	Link Control Procedure
LCP	Local Control Point
LCQ	Logical Channel Queue
LCS	Large Capacity Storage
LCU	Loop Control Unit
LD	Light Detail
LD	Logical Design
LD	Logical Diagram
LD	Long Distance
LDA	Logical Device Address
LDM	Limited Distance Modem
LDM	Local Data Manager
LDO	Logical Device Order
LDT	Logical Device Table
LDU	Line Drive Unit
LE	Logical Element
LE	Loop Error
LE	Low Energy
LED	Light Emitting Diode
lex	Lexicon
LF	Line Feed
LF	Logical Function
LF	Loss Factor
LF	Low Filter
LF	Low Frequency
lft	Left
lg	Large
LG	Line Generator
LGN	Logical Group Number
LH	Left Hand
LIC	Last In Chain
lic	License
LIC	Linear Integrated Circuit
LIF	Line Interface Feature
LIFO	Last In First Out
lim	Limit

ling	Linguistics
liq	Liquid
LISA	Linked Index Sequential Access
lit	Literal
lit	Literally
LIT	Load Initial Table
LL	Leased Line
LL	Local Line
LL	Low Level
LLG	Logical Line Group
LLL	Low Level Language
LM	Load Module
ln	Lane
LNB	Local Name Base
LNT	Low Noise Tape
loc	Local
loc	Location
log	Logarithm
long	Longitude
LOP	Line Oriented Protocol
LOR	Level Of Repair
LOS	Loss Of Signal
LP	Lead Programmer
LP	Light Pen
LP	Line Printer
LP	Linear Programming
LP	Live Preview
LP	Load Point
LP	Longitudinal Parity
LPA	Link Pack Area
LPB	Load Program Block
LPC	Linear Predictive Coding
LPI	Lines Per Inch
LPM	Lines Per Minute
LPN	Logical Page Number
LPS	Linear Programming System
LPS	Lines Per Second
LPU	Language Processor Unit
LQP	Letter Quality Printer
LR	Left to Right
LR	Limit Register
LR	Limit Response
LR	Logical Record
LRC	Longitudinal Redundancy Check
LRCC	Longitudinal Redundancy Check Character
LS	Least Significant
LS	Low Speed
LSB	Least Significant Bit
LSC	Least Significant Character

LSC	Loop Station Connector
LSD	Language for Systems Development
LSD	Line Signal Detector
LSD	List Significant Digit
LSI	Large Scale Integration
LSID	Local Session Identification
LSP	Loop Splice Plate
LSQA	Local System Queue Area
LSR	Local Shared Resources
LSS	Loop Surge Suppresser
LST	Local Standard Time
LSU	Local Store Unit
LT	Less Than
lt	Light
LTD	Line Transfer Device
ltd	Limited
LTH	Logical Track Header
LTOC	Lowest Total Overall Cost
LTPL	Long Term Procedural Language
ltr	Letter
LTU	Line Termination Unit
LTWA	Log Tape Write Ahead
LU	Logical Unit
LUB	Logical Unit Block
LV	Luncheon Voucher
LWA	Last Word Address
LWASR	Letter Writing with Automatic Send-Receive
LWC	Loop Wiring Concentrator

MA	Magnetic Amplifier
MA	Maintenance Agreement
ma	Milliampere
MAC	Machine Aide Cognition
MAC	Maintenance Allocation Chart
MAC	Multiple Access Computer
MAC	Multiple Access Computing
mach	Machine
MACS	Modular Application Customizing System
MAD	Mean Absolute Deviation
MAE	Memory Access Extension
mag	Magazine
MAI	Multiple Access Interface
maint	Maintenance
MAL	Macro-Assembly Language

MAL	Maximum Acceptable Load
MAL	Memory Access Logic
MAM	Memory Allocation Manager
man	Manual
MAP	Macro-Assembly Program
MAP	Maintenance Analysis Procedures
MAP	Memory Allocation and Protection
MAR	Memory Address Register
MAT	Memory Address Test
math	Mathematics
MAU	Media Access Unit
max	Maximum
mb	Megabyte
MBI	Memory Bank Interface
MBO	Management By Objectives
MBPS	Millions of Bits Per Second
MBX	Management By Exception
MBZ	Must Be Zero
MC	Magnetic Card
MC	Management Committee
MC	Master Control
MC	Memory Control
MCAR	Machine Check Analysis and Recording
MCC	Magnetic Card Code
MCC	Master Control Code
MCH	Machine Check Handler
mch	Megacharacter
MCI	Machine Check Interruption
MCI	Monitor Call Instruction
MCL	Monitor Control Language
MCM	Memory Control Module
MCP	Master Control Program
MCP	Message Control Program
MCRR	Machine Check Recording and Recovery
MCU	Magnetic Card Unit
MCU	Microprocessor Control Unit
mcz	Mechanized
MDF	Main Distribution Frame
MDL	Magnetic Delay Line
MDR	Magnetic Document Reader
MDR	Mark Document Reader
MDS	Maintenance Data System
MDS	Microprocessor Development System
MDS	Modular Data System
MDT	Mean Down Time
MDTS	Modular Data Transaction System
MDY	Month Day Year
ME	Manufacturing Engineering
ME	Memory Element

meas	Measure
MEB	Modem Evaluation Board
mech	Mechanical
meg	Megabyte
mem	Memory
memo	Memorandum
MES	Mapping and Earth Science
MES	Miscellaneous Equipment Specification
mesg	Message
met	Metropolitan
MF	Master File
MF	Medium Frequency
MF	Multi-Frequency
MFCM	Multi-Function Card Machine
MFCU	Multi-Function Card Unit
mfd	Manufactured
MFD	Master File Directory
MFG	Message Flow Graph
MFH	Magnetic Film Handler
MFM	Modified Frequency Modulation
MFPE	Minimum Final Prediction Error
mfr	Manufacturer
MFR	Multi-Frequency Receiver
MFS	Message Format Service
mfst	Manifest
mg	Milligram
MGP	Multiple Goal Programming
mgr	Manager
mgt	Management
MH	Message Handler
MHD	Moving Head Disc
MHP	Message Handling Processor
MHS	Magnetic Hand Scanner
MHS	Multiple Host Support
MI	Magnetic Instability
MI	Maintenance Interface
MI	Memory Interface
mi	Mile
MIB	Member Information Bank
MIC	Message Identification Code
MIC	Middle In Chain
MIC	Monolithic Integrated Circuit
MICR	Magnetic Ink Character Recognition
MICS	Management Information and Control System
MID	Message Input Descriptor
mid	Middle
MIH	Missing Interruption Handler
milit	Military
MIM	Modem Interface Module

min	Minimum
min	Minute
MIP	Material In Process
MIP	Mixed Integer Programming
MIPS	Millions of Instructions Per Seconds
MIR	Memory Input Register
MIS	Management Information Service
MIS	Management Information System
MIS	Manufacturing Information System
MIS	Medical Information System
MIS	Multistage Information System
misc	Miscellaneous
MIT	Master Instruction Tape
MIU	Modem Interface Unit
ML	Machine Language
ML	Memory Layout
ML	Memory Location
ml	Milliliter
MLC	Magnetic Ledger Card
MLC	Medium Level Center
MLE	Microprocessor Language Editor
MLP	Multiple Line Printing
MLR	Multiple Line Reading
MLT	Monolithic Logic Technology
MLU	Memory Logic Unit
MM	Main Memory
MM	Mass Memory
MM	Memory Module
mm	Millimeter
MMS	Manufacturing Monitoring System
MMU	Memory Management Unit
MN	Message Number
MNC	Multi-National Company
MNOS	Metal Nitride Oxide Silicon
MO	Manually Operated
MO	Memory Output
MO	Modus Operandi
MO	Money Order
mo	Month
MOD	Message Output Descriptor
mod	Moderate
mod	Modification
MOL	Machine Oriented Language
MOR	Memory Output Register
MOS	Memory Oriented System
MOS	Metal Oxide Semiconductor
MP	Multi-Processor
MP	Multi-Purpose
mp	Microprocessor

MPC	Multi-Processor Controller
MPP	Message Processing Program
MPPS	Message Processing Procedure Specification
MPS	Mathematical Programming System
MPS	Multi-Programming System
MPS	Multiple Partition Support
MPSX	Mathematical Programming System Extended
MRA	Multiple Regression Analysis
MRL	Machine Representation Language
MRM	Machine Readable Material
MRO	Multi-Region Operation
MRP	Machine Readable Passport
MRP	Manufacturing Resource Planning
MRP	Material Requirements Planning
MRP	Multiple Requested Program
MRR	Multiple Response Resolver
MS	Main Storage
MS	Management Science
ms	Manuscript
MS	Margin of Safety
MS	Mark Sensing
MS	Mass Storage
MS	Master Scheduler
MS	Metric System
MS	Momentary Switch
MSA	Mass Storage Adapter
MSB	Most Significant Bit
MSC	Mass Storage Control
MSCF	Multiple Systems Coupling Feature
MSD	Most Significant Digit
MSDB	Main Storage Data Base
MSF	Mass Storage Facility
msg	Message
MSHP	Maintain System History Program
MSI	Medium Scale Integration
MSNF	Multi-System Network Facility
MSP	Most Significant Position
MSR	Magnetic Stripe Reader
MSS	Mass Storage System
MSS	Magnetic Slot Scanner
MSSF	Monitoring and System Support Facility
MST	Monolithic Systems Technology
MSU	Modern Sharing Unit
MSV	Minimum Starting Voltage
MSVC	Mass Storage Volume Control
MT	Magnetic Tape
MT	Mechanical Translation
MT	Machine Translation
MTA	Multiple Terminal Access

MTBC	Mean Time Between Calls
MTBF	Mean Time Between Failures
MTBM	Mean Time Between Maintenance
MTBO	Mean Time Between Overhauls
MTC	Magnetic Tape Controller
MTF	Minimum Toggle Frequency
mtge	Mortgage
MTH	Magnetic Tape Handler
MTOS	Magnetic Tape Operating System
mtr	Monitor
MTTA	Mean Time To Arrive
MTTF	Mean Time To Failure
MTTR	Mean Time To Repair
MTU	Magnetic Tape Unit
MU	Memory Unit
MU	Mobile Unit
mu	Multiuser
MUL	Master Urgency List
multl	Multiple
muni	Municipal
MUST	Message User Service Transcriber
MUT	Module Under Test
mux	Multiplexer
MV	Mean Variation
mv	Multivolt
MVS	Multiple Virtual Storage
MW	Man Week
MY	Man-Year
myth	Mythology

NA	No Action
NA	No Activity
NA	Not Accurate
NA	Not Active
NA	Not Actual
NA	Not Applicable
NA	Not Authorized
NA	Not Available
NA	Numerical Aperture
NAA	Noise Analysis Approach
NAB	National Association of Broadcasters
NAC	Network Access Controller
NAD	No Apparent Defect
NAI	Net Annual Inflow

NAK	Negative Acknowledge Character
NAPLS	North American Presentation Level Protocol Syntax
NAR	No Action Required
NAS	Network Administration Station
NAS	National Academy of Sciences
NASA	National Aeronautics and Space Administration
NASD	National Association of Securities Dealers
NAT	No Action Taken
nat	National
NATTS	National Association for Trade and Technical Schools
NAU	Network Addressable Unit
naut	Nautical
NB	Narrow Band
NB	Noise Block
NBP	Name-Binding Protocol
nbr	Number
NBS	National Bureau of Standards
NC	Narrow Coverage
NC	Network Control
NC	Normally Closed
NC	Numerical Control
NCC	National Computing Conference
NCC	National Control Center
NCC	National Computer Conference
NCCF	Network Communications Control Facility
NCI	Non-Coded Information
NCP	Network Control Program
NCPS	National Commission on Product Safety
NCR	No Carbon Required
NCS	Network Control Station
NCU	Network Control Unit
ND	No Date
ND	Normal Detail
ND	Not Desirable
NDC	Normalized Device Coordinates
NDL	Network Definition Language
NDPS	National Data Processing Service
NDRC	Non Destructive Read Character
NDRO	Non Destructive Read Out
NDS	Network Development System
NE	No Equal
NEB	National Enterprise Board
NEC	National Electrical Code
NEDC	National Economic Development Council
neg	Negative
NEMA	National Electrical Manufacturer's Association
NEP	Never-Ending Program
net	Network
NF	Normal Form

NFC	Not Favorably Considered
NFF	No Fault Found
NFP	Network Facilities Package
NFPA	National Fire Protection Association
NHI	National Health Insurance
NHS	National Health Service
nhz	Nanohertz
NIA	No Input Acknowledge
NIB	Node Initialization Block
NIC	Network Information Center
NIF	Network Information File
NIH	Not Invented Here
NIH -	National Institute of Health
NIM	Network Interface Machine
NIP	Non Impact Printer
NIP	Nucleus Initialization Program
NIRS	National Information Research Institute
NIS	Network Information Services
NIT	Nearly Intelligent Terminal
NIU	Network Interface Unit
NJE	Network Job Entry
NJI	Network Job Interface
NL	New Line
NLQ	Near Letter Quality
NLT	Not Later Than
NLT	Not Less Than
NMA	National Microfilm Association
NMAA	National Machine Accountants Association
NMF	New Master File
nna	Nanoampere
no	Number
NO	Normally Open
NOF	National Optical Font
nom	Nominative
NOMA	National Office Management Association
NOPA	National Office Products Association
norm	Normal
NOS	Network Operating System
NOSP	Network Operation Support Program
NPC	Non Printing Character
NPDA	Network Problem Determination Application
NPDN	Nordic Public Data Network
NPL	National Physical Laboratory
NPR	Numerical Position Readout
NPS	Network Processing Supervisor
nr	Near
NRDC	National Research and Development Council
NRMA	National Retail Merchant Association
NRT	Non Requester Terminal

NRZ	Non Return to Zero
NS	Network Services
NS	New Signal
NSA	National Security Agency
NSC	Network Switching Center
NSF	National Science Foundation
NSN	National Stock Number
NSP	Network Services Protocol
NSPE	Network Services Procedure Error
NSR	No Slot Release
NSR	Normal Service Request
NSTC	Not Subject To Call
NTA	National Telecommunications Agency
NTC	National Telecommunications Conference
NTE	Not To Exceed
NTF	Network Transfer Function
NTF	No Trouble Found
NTO	Network Terminal Option
NTP	Network Terminal Protocol
NTR	Nine Thousand Remote
NTSC	National Television Standard Code
NTU	Network Terminating Unit
NUA	Network Users Association
NUL	No Upper Limit
num	Numeral
NVRAM	Non Volatile Random Access Memory
NVT	Network Virtual Terminal
NWD	Network Wide Directory
NWDS	Network Wide Directory System
NXA	Nodal Exchange Area
NY	Not Yield
NZSG	Non Zero Sum Game

OA	Office Automation
OA	Operating Authorization
OAAU	Orthogonal Array Arithmetic Unit
OAF	Origin Address Field
OAR	Office of Aerospace Research
OAR	Operator Authorization Record
OAS	Organizational Accounting Structure
OB	Official Business
OB	Output Buffer
OBC	On-Board Computer
obj	Object

OBR	Optical Bar-code Reader
obs	Obsolete
OBS	Optical Beam Scanner
OC	Office Copy
OC	Official Classification
OC	Open Circuit
OC	Operating Characteristic
OC	Operation Code
OC	Operation Control
OC	Optical Communication
OC	Order Card
occ	Occupation
OCC	Operator Control Command
occas	Occasionally
OCCF	Operator Communication Control Facility
OCDS	Output Command Data Set
OCF	Operator Console Facility
OCL	Operator Control Language
OCL	Output Capacity Loading
OCP	Order Code Processor
OCR	Optical Character Reading
OCR	Optical Character Recognition
OCRIT	Optical Character Recognizing Intelligent Terminal
oct	Octal
OCV	Open Circuit Voltage
ODB	Output Data Buffer
ODD	Optical Data Digitizer
ODE	Ordinary Differential Equation
ODP	Optical Data Processing
ODR	Optical Data Recognition
ODR	Original Data Record
ODT	Octal Debugging Technique
OEA	Operator Error Analysis
OED	Opto Electronic Display
OEF	Origin Element Field
OEM	Original Equipment Manufacturer
of	Official
of	Overflow
og	Outgoing
oh	Overhead
OI	Operating Instructions
OIC	Only-In-Chain
OIC	Operations Instrumentation Coordinator
OIC	Operator Instruction Chart
OIS	Office Information System
OL	On Line
OL	Open Loop
OL	Operating Location
OLE	Object-Linking and Embedding

OLRT	On-Line Real Time
OLTEP	On-Line Test Executive Program
OLTS	On-Line Test System
OLTT	On-Line Terminal Test
OM	Office Manager
OM	Office Master
OM	Operating Memory
OM	Operation Manual
OM	Output Module
OMC	Open Magnetic Circuit
OMR	Optical Mark Reading
ON	Operation Number
op	Operation
op	Optional
OP	Overflow Position
OPD	Office Product Division
OPD	Overcurrent Protective Device
OPM	Operations Per Minute
opnl	Operational
opp	Opposite
OPR	Optical Page Reader
ops	Operations
OPS	Operations Per Second
OPUR	Object Program Utility Routine
OQL	Outgoing Quality Level
OR	On Return
OR	Operation Record
OR	Operational Research
OR	Over Run
ord	Order
ord	Ordinary
org	Organization
orig	Originally
ORS	Optimal Real Storage
ORSA	Operations Research Society of America
OS	Office System
OS	Old Style
OS	On Schedule
OS	Operating System
OS	Operational Sequence
OS	Optical Scanning
OS	Optimum Size
OS	Order Sheet
os	Outstanding
OSA	Open Systems Architecture
OSAM	Overflow Sequential Access Method
OSB	Operational Status Bit
osc	Oscillator
OSE	Operational Support Equipment

OSHA	Occupational Safety and Health Administration
OSI	Open Systems Interconnection
OSN	Output Sequence Number
OSS	Operating System Supervisor
OST	Operator Station Task
OSU	Operational Switching Unit
OT	Office of Telecommunications
OT	On Time
OT	On Track
OT	Operating Time
OTA	Office of Technology Assessment
OTB	Off-Track Betting
OTF	Optical Transfer Function
OTR	Operating Temperature Range
out	Outgoing
ovld	Overload
OW	Ordinary Wave
OWC	One Way Communication
oz	Ounce

PA	Pending Availability
PA	Problem Analysis
PA	Product Assurance
PA	Product Attention
PA	Program Access
PA	Program Analysis
PA	Public Address
PAB	Primary Application Block
PABX	Private Automatic Branch Exchange
PAC	Planned Availability Concept
PAC	Primary Address Code
PAC	Program Authorized Credentials
PAC	Project Analysis and Control
PAC	Performance Analysis and Control
PAD	Packet Assembly Disassembly
PAL	Phase Alternation Line
PAL	Programmable Array Logic
PAM	Pulse Amplitude Modulation
par	Paragraph
paren	Parentheses
parm	Parameter
PAS	Processed Array Signal
PAST	Process Accessible Segment Table
pat	Patent

931046

PAT	Peripheral Allocation Table
PAT	Programmers Aptitude Test
patd	Patented
patt	Pattern
PAV	Program Activation Vector
PAX	Private Automatic Exchange
PAYE	Pay As You Earn
PB	Page Buffer
PB	Program Base
PBA	Printed Board Assembly
PBX	Private Branch Exchange
PC	Path Control
pc	Percentage
PC	Permanently Connected
PC	Personal Computer
pc	Photoconductor
PC	Plug Compatible
PC	Portable Computer
PC	Printed Circuit
PC	Process Control
PC	Production Control
PC	Production Cost
PC	Professional Corporation
PCA	Primary Communication Attachment
PCA	Printed Circuit Analyzer
PCA	Printed Circuit Assembly
PCA	Pulse Counter Adapter
PCAM	Partitioned Content Addressable Memory
PCAM	Punched Card Accounting Machine
PCB	Page Control Block
PCB	Printed Circuit Board
PCB	Process Control Block
PCB	Program Communication Block
PCB	Program Control Block
PCBS	Printed Circuit Board Socket
PCD	Partition Control Descriptor
PCD	Pre Configured Definition
PCD	Production Common Digitizer
PCD	Program Control Document
PCE	Processing and Control Element
PCF	Program Complex File
PCF	Program Control Facility
pch	Punch
PCI	Program Check Interruption
PCI	Program Controlled Interruption
PCK	Phase Control Keyboard
PCL	Print Control Language
PCL	Process Control Language
PCM	Plug Compatible Manufacturers

PCM	Pulse Coded Modulation
PCM	Punch Card Machine
PCO	Program Change Order
PCP	Peripheral Control Pulse
PCP	Preliminary Cost Proposal
PCP	Primary Control Program
PCP	Process Control Program
PCP	Program Change Proposal
PCR	Peripheral Control Routine
PCS	Print Contrast Signal
PCS	Project Control System
PCT	Partition Control Table
PCU	Peripheral Control Unit
PCU	Power Control Unit
PCU	Program Control Unit
PCU	Punch Card Unit
pd	Paid
PD	Panel Display
PD	Physical Distribution
PD	Potential Difference
PD	Procedure Division
PD	Process Descriptor
PD	Product Design
PDA	Physical Device Address
PDC	Parallel Data Controller
PDC	Programmable Desk Calculator
PDDB	Product Definition Data Base
PDL	Process Design Language
PDL	Program Design Language
PDL	Push Down List
PDM	Pulse Duration Modulation
PDN	Public Data Network
PDS	Partitioned Data Set
PE	Parity Error
PE	Period Ending
PE	Phase Encoded
PE	Picture Element
PE	Probable Error
PE	Processing Element
PE	Pulse Encoding
PEC	Page End Character
PEC	Program Element Code
PEC	Program Exception Code
PECOS	Project Evaluation and Cost Optimization Systems
PEL	Picture Element
PEM	Program Execution Monitor
PEP	Partitioned Emulation Programming
per	Period
PER	Program Event Recording

perm	Permanent
pers	Personal
PERT	Program Evaluation and Review Technique
PF	Parallel Feed
Pfd	Preferred
PFR	Power Fail Recovery
PFT	Page Frame Table
pgm	Program
PGT	Program Global Table
ph	Phase
PHB	Program Header Block
photo	Photograph
phr	Phrase
PI	Photoelectric Inspection
PI	Program Isolation
PI	Programmed Instruction
PIA	Peripheral Interface Adapter
PIC	Position Independent Code
PIC	Priority Intercept Controller
PIC	Production Inventory Control
PIC	Program Information Code
PIC	Program Interrupt Control
PICS	Production Information and Control System
PID	Personal Identification Device
PIM	Personal Information Manager
PIM	Processor Interface Module
PIN	Personal Identification Number
PIO	Programmed Input/Output
PIO	Peripheral Input/Output
PIOCS	Physical Input/Output Control System
PIRV	Programmed Interrupt Request Vector
PIU	Path Information Unit
PIU	Peripheral Interface Unit
pkg	Package
PL	Periodic Line
PL	Pilot Lamp
pl	Plural
pl	Plus
PL	Programming Language
PLA	Programmable Logic Array
PLC	Programming Language Committee
PLCB	Program List Control Block
plcy	Policy
PLO	Phase-Locked Oscillator
PLPS	Presentation Level Protocol Standard
PLR	Program Library Release
PLS	Picture Line Standard
PM	Afternoon (Post Meridiem)
PM	Preventive Maintenance

PM	Program Mode
PM	Phase Modulation
PMBX	Private Manual Branch Exchange
PMCT	Program Management Control Table
PMF	Performance Measurement Facility
PMl	Personnel Management Information
PMMU	Paged-Memory-Management Unit
PMS	Public Message Service
PMS	Project Management System
PMTS	Predetermined Motion Time System
PMX	Private Manual Exchange
PN	Part Number
PNA	Project Network Analysis
PNR	Passenger Name Record
PO	Purchase Order
PO	Post Office
POF	Programmed Operator Facility
POF	Point-Of-Failure
POH	Power-On Hours
pol	Polish
POL	Problem-Oriented Language
POl	Program Operator Interface
POLE	Point Of Last Environment
POM	Printer Output Microfilm
pop	Popular
POP	Project Optimization Procedures
POS	Point Of Sale
POS	Pascal Operating System
poss	Possessive
POTS	Plain Old Telephone Service
PPA	Protected Partition Area
PPBS	Planning Programming and Budgeting System
ppd	Postpaid
PPDF	Portable Postscript-Document Format
PPE	Problem Program Evaluator
PPE	Problem Program Efficiency
PPI	Plate Power Input
PPl	Pulses Per Inch
PPM	Pulse Position Modulation
PPS	Plate Power Supply
PPS	Pulses Per Second
PPSN	Public Packet-Switched Network
PQA	Protected Queue Area
PRC	Primary Return Code
PRC	Program Required Credentials
PRC	Postal Rate Commission
pref	Preface
PRF	Pulse Repetition Frequency
prio	Priority

priv	Private
prl	Parallel
proc	Processing
procd	Procedure
prod	Product
proj	Project
PROLOG	Programming Logic
PROM	Programmable Read-Only Memory
prot	Protect
prov	Province
PRR	Pulse Repetition Rate
prt	Printer
PS	Pace Setter
PS	Packet Switch
PS	Picture System
ps	Postscript
PS	Power Supply
PS	Preliminary Study
PS	Process Specification
PS	Processor Status
PS	Program Start
PS	Programming System
PS	Protect Status
PS	Presentation Services
PSA	Process Service Area
PSA	Peripherals Suppliers Association
PSB	Program Specification Block
PSCB	Presentation Services Command
PSCF	Primary System Control Facility
PSE	Packet Switching Exchange
pseud	Pseudonym
PSG	Planning System Generator
PSI	Peripheral Subsystem Interface
PSI	Personal Security Identifier
PSI	Pounds per Square Inch
PSI	Program Status Information
PSK	Phase Shift Keying
PSM	Peak Selector Memory
PSM	Power Supply Module
PSM	Production Systems Management
PSM	Productive Standard Minute
PSM	Program Support Monitor
PSM	Proportional Spacing Machine
PSN	Print Sequence Number
PSN	Public Switched Network
PSP	Packet Switching Processor
PSR	Performance Summary Report
PSR	Processor State Register
PSR	Program Status Register

PSR	Program Status Report
PSR	Programming Support Representative
PSRR	Product and Support Requirements Request
PSS	Packet Switching Services
PSS	Planned Systems Schedule
PSS	Printer Storage System
PSS	Process Switching Services
PST	Priority Selection Table
PST	Program Synchronization Table
PSTN	Public Switched Telephone Network
PSU	Packet Switching Unit
PSU	Port Sharing Unit
PSU	Power Supply Unit
PSU	Processor Service Unit
PSU	Processor Speed Up
PSU	Processor Storage Unit
PSU	Program Storage Unit
PSV	Program Status Vector
PSW	Processor Status Word
PSW	Program Status Word
pt	Part
PT	Photoelectric Timer
PT	Picture Transmission
pt	Point
PT	Processing Time
PT	Processor Terminal
PT	Punched Table
ptd	Printed
PTE	Page Table Entry
PTF	Program Temporary Fix
PTM	Phase Time Modulation
PTM	Programmable Terminal Multiplexer
PTM	Pulse Transmission Mode
PTP	Paper Tape Punch
PTP	Point To Point
PTR	Paper Tape Reader
PTTC	Paper Tape Transmission Code
PTW	Page Table Word
PU	Peripheral Unit
PU	Physical Unit
PU	Processing Unit
PUB	Physical Unit Block
pub	Publication
PUCP	Physical Unit Control Point
PVS	Program Validation Services
pvt	Private
PW	Printed Wiring
PW	Processor Write
pw	Password

PWA	Printed Wire Assembly
PWM	Pulse Width Modulation
pwr	Power
PWS	Program Work Statement
PWS	Programmer Work Station

QA	Quality Assessment
QB	Quick Batch
QBE	Query By Example
QC	Quality Control
QCB	Queue Control Block
QCS	Quality Control Specification
QECB	Queued Element Control Block
QF	Quality Factor
QISAM	Queued Indexed Sequential Access Method
QMDO	Quality Material development Objectives
QNS	Quantity Not Sufficient
QOH	Quantity On Hand
QPL	Qualified Products List
QR	Quality and Reliability
QRC	Quick Reaction Communication
QS	Query Similarity
QS	Query System
QSAM	Queued Sequential Access Method
QSL	Queue Search Limit
qt	Quart
QTAM	Queued Terminal Access Method
QTP	Quality Test Plan
QTR	Quality Technical Requirement
qty	Quantity
qual	Quality
QXI	Queue Executive Interface

RA	Random Access
RA	Read Amplifier
RA	Record Address
RA	Refer to Accepter
RA	Repair Action
RA	Repeat to Address

RA	Return Address
RA	Rotary Assembly
RAD	Random Access Device
RAIR	Remote Access Immediate Response
RAM	Random Access Measurement
RAM	Random Access Memory
RAM	Remote Access Monitor
RAM	Resident Access Method
RAP	Response Analysis Program
RAR	Rapid Access Recording
RAS	Random Access Storage
RB	Relay Block
RBA	Relative Byte Address
RBP	Registered Business Programmer
RBT	Region Control Task
RBT	Remote Batch Terminal
RC	Reader Code
RC	Receiver Card
RC	Remote Computer
RC	Remote Control
RC	Retrieval Center
RCA	Reaction Control Assembly
RCA	Remote Control Adapter
RCB	Request Control Block
RCB	Resource Control Block
rcd	Record
RCF	Reader's Comment Form
RCF	Remote Call Forwarding
RCF	Retail Computer Facilities
RCP	Recognition and Control Processor
RCS	Reloadable Control Store
RCT	Region Control Task
RD	Read Data
RD	Receive Data
RD	Required Data
rd	Road
rd	Round
RDC	Remote Data Collection
RDF	Record Definition Field
RDH	Remote Device Handler
rdj	Readjustment
RDP	Remote Data Processor
rdr	Reader
RDT	Resource Definition Table
RE	Request Element
rec	Recover
recd	Received
ref	Reference
reg	Registered

regs	Regulations
rej	Reject
rel	Relative
rep	Reply
repr	Representation
RES	Remote Entry Services
res	Residence
resrt	Restart
REU	Ready Extension Unit
REU	Remote Entry Unit
rev	Reverse
REW	Read Executive Write
RF	Radio Frequency
RF	Read Forward
RF	Register File
RF	Reliability Factor
RF	Reporting File
RFA	Register Field Address
RFD	Ready For Data
RFI	Radio Frequency Interference
RFI	Ready For Use
RFP	Request For Programming
RFP	Request For Proposal
RFQ	Request For Quotation
rfrsh	Refresh
RFS	Random Filing System
RFT	Request For Test
RGB	Red Green Blue
RGP	Remote Graphics Processor
RH	Relative Humidity
RH	Right Hand
RHS	Right Hand Side
RI	Radio Interface
RI	Register Immediate
RI	Reliability Index
RIA	Regulatory Impact Analysis
RIA	Research Institute of America
RIA	Robot Institute of America
RIDS	Reset Information Data Set
RIF	Relative Importance Factor
RIM	Read-In Mode
RIR	Request Immediate Reply
RJE	Remote Job Entry
RJP	Remote Job Processing
RLA	Remote Loop Adapter
RLL	Run Length Limited
RLM	Resident Load Module
RLR	Record Length Register
RM	Register Memory

rmdr	Remainder
RMM	Read Mostly Memory
RMM	Remote Maintenance Monitor
RMS	Random Mass Storage
RMS	Record Management Service
RMS	Record Management System
RMS	Recovery Management Support
RMS	Resource Management System
RNX	Restricted Numeric Exchange
RO	Read Only
RO	Receive Only
RO	Register Output
ROI	Return On Investment
ROM	Read Only Memory
RON	Run Occurrence Number
ROS	Read Only Storage
ROS	Resident Operating System
ROTR	Receive Only Typing Reperforator
RPC	Regional Processing Center
RPE	Relative Price Effect
RPG	Report Program Generator
RPL	Request Parameter List
RPM	Revolutions Per Minute
RPN	Reverse Polish Quotation
RPQ	Request for Price Quotation
RPS	Remote Printing System
RPS	Revolutions Per Second
RPS	Rotational Position Sensing
rpt	Repeat
RPU	Remote Processing Unit
RPW	Running Process Word
RQE	Reply Queue Element
RR	Receive Ready
RRN	Relative Record Number
RRN	Remote Request Number
RS	Reader Stop
RS	Real Storage
RS	Record Separator
RS	Register Select
RS	Remote Site
RS	Remote System
RS	Request to Send
RSAM	Relative Sequential Access Method
RSCS	Remote Spooling Communications Subsystem
RSDS	Relative Sequential Data Set
RSM	Real Storage Management
RSP	Record Select Program
RSP	Remote Support Facility
RSPT	Real Storage Page Table

RSS	Relational Storage System
RSS	Resource Security System
RSS	Routing and Switching System
rst	Reset
RT	Real Time
RT	Receive Timing
RT	Receiver-Transmitter
RT	Register Transfer
RT	Remote Terminal
rt	Right
RT	Run Time
RTAM	Remote Telecommunications Access Method
RTAM	Remote Terminal Access Method
rte	Route
RTI	Real-Time Interface
RTI	Referred To Input
RTL	Resistor Transistor Logic
RTM	Real-Time Monitor
RTM	Register Transfer Module
RTM	Registered Trade Mark
RTMP	Routing Table Maintenance Protocol
rtn	Return
RTOS	Real-Time Operating System
RTS	Reactive Terminal Service
RTS	Real-Time System
RTS	Remote Terminal Supervisor
RTS	Remote Terminal System
RTS	Requested To Send
rts	Rights
RVA	Recorded Voice Announcement
RVI	Reverse Interrupt
RVT	Resource Vector Table
RWI	Read-Write-Initialize
RWM	Read/Write Memory
RWO	Right Wrong Omits
RWO	Routine Work Order
RWR	Read Writer Register
RZ	Return to Zero
RZM	Return to Zero Mark

SA	Sample Array
SA	Scaling Amplifier
SA	Sense Amplifier
SA	Shift Advance

SA	Signal Analyzer
SA	Stack Access
SA	Store Address
SA	Synchro Amplifier
SA	System Address
SA	System Analysis
SAA	Service Action Analysis
SAA	Slot Array Antenna
SAB	Secondary Application Block
SAB	Session Awareness Block
SAB	Stack Access Block
SAB	System Advisory Board
SAC	Servo Adapter Coupler
SAC	Single Address Code
SAC	Special Area Code
SAC	Store Access Control
SAC	Store And Clear
SAD	System Analysis Drawing
SADT	Structure Analysis and Design Technique
SAF	Segment Address Field
SAG	Systems Analysis Group
SAL	Service Action Log
SAL	Structured Assembly Language
SAL	Systems Assembly Language
SAM	Sequential Access Memory
SAM	Sequential Access Method
SAM	System Activity Monitor
SAM	Systems Adapter Module
SAP	Share Assembly Program
SAP	Structural Analysis Program
SAR	Source Address Register
SAR	Storage Address Register
SASE	Self-Addressed Stamped Envelope
SAT	System Access Technique
SAU	Standard Advertising Unit
SAVT	Secondary Address Vector Table
SAW	Surface Acoustic Wave
SAYE	Save As You Earn
SB	Stabilized Breakdown
SB	Stack Base
SB	Statistical Bulletins
SB	Straight Binary
SBA	Shared Batch Area
SBA	Small Business Administrator
SBA	Strategic Business Area
SBC	Single Board Computer
SBC	Small Business Computer
SBS	Satellite Business Systems
SBS	Small Business System

SBS	Special Block Sale
SBS	Subscript Character
SC	Satellite Computer
SC	Selector Channel
SC	Sequence Controller
SC	Sequence Counter
SC	Session Control
SC	Short Circuit
SC	Single Column
SC	Single Counter
SC	Source Code
SC	Statistical Control
SC	Storage Capacity
SC	Subscriber Computer
SC	Symbolic Code
SC	System Controller
SCA	System Control Area
SCB	Station Control Block
SCB	String Control Byte
SCC	Specialized Common Carriers
SCD	System Contents Directory
SCF	System Control Facility
sch	Schedule
sci	Science
SCI	Science Citation Index
SCL	System Control Language
scn	Scanner
SCP	Supervisory Control Program
SCP	System Control Program
SCR	Scan Control Register
SCR	Silicon Controlled Rectifier
SCR	Single Character Recognition
SCR	Software Change Report
SCR	System Change Request
SCS	Small Computer System
SCS	Society for Computer Simulation
SCSI	Small Computer Systems Interface
SCT	Special Character Table
SCT	System Configuration Table
sd	Said
SD	Send Data
SD	Single Density
SD	Switch Driver
SD	System Development
SD	Systems Design
SDA	Source Data Automation
SDI	Selective Dissemination of Information
SDI	Serial Data In
SDL	System Design Language

SDL	System Directory List
SDLC	Synchronous Data Link Control
SDO	Serial Data Out
SDR	Statistical Data Recorded
SDR	System Definition Record
SDU	Source Data Utility
SDW	Segment Descriptor Word
SDX	Satellite Data Exchange
SE	Sign Extended
SE	Single End
SE	Single Entry
SE	Software Engineering
SE	Special Equipment
SE	Standard Error
SE	System Element
SE	System Extension
SEA	Self-Extracting Archives
sec	Second
SEC	Security and Exchange Commission
SECAM	Sequential Color with Memory
seg	Segment
sel	Select
SEP	Separate Element Pricing
seq	Sequence
ser	Serial
ser	Series
SERC	Science and Engineering Research Council
SEREP	System Error Record Editing Program
SET	Selective Employment Tax
sev	Several
SF	Safety Factor
SF	Scale Factor
SF	Short Format
SF	Signal Frequency
SF	Skip Flag
SF	Special Facilities
SF	Square Foot
SF	Stack Full
SFC	Sector File Controller
SG	Scanning Gate
SG	Single Ground
SG	Specific Gravity
SG	Symbol Generator
SG	System Gain
sgd	Signed
SGJP	Satellite Graphic Job Processor
SGL	System Generation Language
SGP	Statistics Generation Program
SHA	Software Houses Association

shf	Shift
SHF	Super High Frequency
shr	Share
SHY	Syllable Hyphen Character
SI	Scientific Instrument
SI	Serial Input
SI	Signal Interface
SI	Single Instruction
SI	Special Instruction
SI	Square Inch
si	Superimpose
SI	System Integration
SIA	Semiconductor Industry Association
SIA	Software Industry Association
SIA	Standard Interface Adapter
SIAM	Society for Industrial and Applied Mathematics
SIAM	System Integrated Access Method
SIB	Screen Image Buffer
SIB	Serial Interface Board
SIB	Session Information Block
SIB	System Interface Bus
SIC	Special Interest Committee
SIC	Standard Industrial Classification
SID	Society for Information Display
SIDF	Standard Interchange Data Form
SIF	Storage Interface Facility
sig	Signal
SIG	Special Interest Group
SII	Standard Individual Identifier
SIL	Store Interface Link
sim	Simulator
SIMD	Single Instruction Multiple Data
SIMM	Single In-line Memory Module
sing	Singular
SIO	Serial Input/Output
SIP	Simulated Input Processor
SIP	Single In-line Package
SIP	System Initialize Program
SIR	Selective Information Retrieval
SIR	Semantic Information Retrieval
SIS	Scientific Information System
SIS	Scientific Instruction Set
SIS	Software Integrated Schedule
SIS	Standard Instruction Set
SIU	System Integration Unit
SJ	Source Jamming
SJCC	Spring Joint Computer Conference
SKU	Stock Keeping Unit
SL	Section List

SL	Shift Left
SL	Simulation Language
SL	Standard Label
SL	Statistical List
SL	Systems Language
SLAP	Subscriber Line Access Protocol
SLC	Single Line Controller
SLC	Subscriber Line Charge
SLC	System Life Cycle
SLD	Straight Line Depreciation
SLD	Synchronous Line Drive
SLIC	Silent Liquid Integral Cooler
SLIC	Subscriber Line Interface Circuit
SLIP	Symmetric List Interpretive Program
SLSI	Super Large Scale Integration
SLSS	System Library Subscription Service
SLT	Solid Logic Technology
SLU	Secondary Logical Unit
SLU	Serial Line Unit
SLU	Source Library Update
SM	Scientific Memorandum
SM	Sequence Monitor
SM	Service Manual
sm	Small
SM	Sort Merge
SM	Special Memo
SM	Structure Memory
SM	Supply Manual
SM	Synchronous Modem
SMD	Storage Module Drive
SME	Society of Manufacturing Engineers
SMF	System Management Facility
SML	Symbolic Machine Language
SMM	Semiconductor Memory Module
SMM	System Management Monitor
SMS	Shared Mass Storage
SMS	Standard Modular System
SMS	System Measurement Software
SN	Sector Number
SN	Sequence Number
SN	Serial Number
SN	Signal Node
SN	Systems Network
SNA	Systems Network Architecture
SNBU	Switched Network Backup
SNF	Sequence Number Field
SNOBOL	String-Oriented Symbolic Language
SO	Send Only
SO	Serial Output

SO	Special Operations
SO	Stop Order
SO	Support Operations
SO	System Operation
SO	Systems Orientation
SOA	Safe Operating Area
SOA	Start Of Address
SOA	State Of Art
soc	Society
SOH	Start Of Header
sol	Solution
SOM	Self Organizing Machine
SOM	Small Office Microfilm
SOM	Start Of Message
SOM	System Operator Manual
SOP	Standard Operating Procedure
SOP	Study Organization Plan
SOR	Single Operator Responsibility
SOS	Silicone On Sapphire
SOS	Sophisticated Operating System
SOS	Start Of Significance
SOS	Station Operator Support
SP	Satellite Processor
SP	Scratch Pad
SP	Send Processor
SP	Sequential Phase
SP	Set Point
SP	Single Precision
SP	Single Programmer
SP	Space Character
SP	Structured Programming
SP	Switch Panel
SP	System Parameter
SP	Systems Programmed
SPA	Scratch Pad Area
SPA	Shared Peripheral Area
SPA	Single Parameter Analysis
SPA	System Programmed Application
SPC	Small Peripheral Controller
SPC	Stored Program Control
SPC	Switching and Processing Center
SPDT	Single Pole Double Throw
spec	Special
SPF	Structured Programming Facility
SPG	Sort Program Generator
SPI	Shared Peripheral Interface
SPI	Single Processor Interface
SPI	Single Program Initiator
SPI	Specific Productivity Index

SPIN	Searchable Physics Information Notice
SPM	Scratch Pad Memory
SPM	Source Program Maintenance
SPM	System Planning Manual
SPN	Switched Public Network
SPPS	Subsystem Program Preparation Support
SPR	Software Problem Report
SPR	Storage Protection Register
spr	Supreme
SPR	System Parameter Record
SPROM	Switched Programmable Read-Only Memory
SPS	String Process System
SPS	Symbolic Program System
SPT	Structured Programming Techniques
SPT	System Parameter Table
sq	Square
SQA	System Queue Area
SQL	Structured Query Language
SR	Scientific Report
SR	Service Record
SR	Special Register
SR	Special Report
SR	Speech Recognition
SR	Standard Requirement
SR	Status Register
SR	Storage Register
SR	Summary Report
SR	System Reader
SRB	Service Request Block
src	Source
SRF	Software Recovery Facility
SRI	Standard Research Institute
SRM	Short Range Modem
SRM	System Resources Manager
SRR	Serially Reusable Resource
SRR	System Requirements Review
SRST	System Resource and Status Table
SRT	Segmentation Register Table
SRT	Single Requester Terminal
SS	Satellite Switched
SS	Satellite System
SS	Save Segment
SS	Selective Signaling
SS	Signal Selector
SS	Single Scan
ss	Steamship
SS	Synchro Standard
SS	System Segment
SSA	Segment Search Argument

SSA	Slave Service Area
SSA	Status Save Area
SSA	Structure Systems Analysis
SSAM	Slave Service Area Module
SSCF	Secondary System Control Facility
SSCP	System Service Control Point
SSDD	Single-Sided Double-Density
SSDR	Supermarket Subsystem Definition Record
SSE	Special Support Equipment
SSE	Switching System Engineer
SSI	Small Scale Integration
SSL	Software Specification Language
SSL	Source Statement library
SSL	Storage Structure Language
SSL	System Specification Language
SSN	Single Stack Number
SSP	System Service Program
SSP	System Status Panel
SSQD	Single-Sided Quad Density
SSR	Software Specification Review
SSR	Solid State Relay
SSR	System Status Report
SSS	Subsystem Support Services
SSSD	Single-Sided Single-Density
SST	System Scheduler Table
ST	Sequence Timer
ST	Special Text
ST	Special Tools
ST	Station Manager
st	State
st	Status
ST	Straight Time
st	Street
ST	Synchronization Table
ST	System Table
ST	System Test
STAIRS	Storage And Information Retrieval System
STC	Serving Test Center
std	Standard
STD	Subscriber Trunk Dialing
STDM	Statistical Time Division Multiplexor
STE	Segment Table Entry
STE	Special Test Equipment
STE	Standard Test Equipment
STE	Subscriber Terminal Equipment
STL	Schottky Transistor Logic
stnd	Standard
STOCS	Small Terminal Oriented Computer Systems
STP	Signal Transfer Point

STP	Stop Character
STR	Segment Table Register
STR	Synchronous Transmit Receive
STR	Synchronous Transmitter Receiver
STRAM	Synchronous Transmit Receive Access Method
STRESS	Structure Engineering System Solver
STST	System Task Set Table
STW	System Tape Writer
STX	Start of Text
SU	Selectable Unit
SU	Signaling Unit
SU	Statute of Uses
SU	Storage Unit
SU	Switching Unit
sub	Subject
supp	Supplement
sur	Surface
sur	Surplus
surv	Survey
SVA	Shared Virtual Area
svc	Service
SVC	Switched Virtual Circuit
SVS	Single Virtual Storage
SVS	Single Virtual System
SVT	System Validation Testing
SVT	System Variable Table
SW	Single Weight
SW	Specific Weight
SW	Status Word
sw	Switch
SWA	Scheduler Work Area
SWA	System Work Area
SWADS	Scheduler Work Area Data Set
SWAMI	Software Aided Multifont Input
swch	Switch
sym	Symbol
SYN	Synchronous Idle Character
syn	Synonym
sync	Synchronous
sys	System

TA	Tape Adapter
TA	Telegraphic Address
TA	Terminal Access

TA	Transactional Analysis
TA	Transfer Address
TAB	Tape Automated Bonding
TAB	Tone Answer Back
TACT	Terminal Activated Channel Test
TAD	Terminal Address Designator
TAD	Time Available for Delivery
TAD	Transaction Applications Driver
TAF	Time And Frequency
TAG	Time Automated Grid
TAM	Task Analysis Method
TAM	Telecommunications Access Method
TAM	Terminal Access Method
tan	Tangent
TAR	Terminal Address Register
TAR	Track Address Register
TAR	Transfer Address Register
TB	Terminal Block
TB	Time Base
TBO	Time Between Overhaul
TC	Tabulating Card
TC	Technical Cooperation
tc	Telecommunications
TC	Terminal Computer
TC	Terminal Control
TC	Test Conductor
TC	Test Coordinator
TC	Time Clock
TC	Transfer Count
TC	Transmission Control
TC	Trunk Control
TCAS	Terminal Control Address Space
TCB	Task Control Block
TCB	Thread Control Block
TCB	Transaction Control Block
TCB	Transfer Control Block
TCF	Terminal Configuration Facility
TCM	Terminal Computer and Multiplexer
TCM	Thermally Control Module
TCU	Terminal Control Unit
TCU	Transmission Control Unit
TD	Tape Drive
TD	Technical Data
TD	Test Data
TD	Time Division
TD	Track Data
TD	Transmit Data
TD	Transmitter Distributor
TDCC	Transformation Data Coordination Committee

TDL	Terminal Display Language
TDL	Transformation Definition Language
TDM	Template Descriptor Memory
TDM	Time Division Multiplexing
TDM	Time Driven Monitor
TDMA	Tape Direct Memory Access
TDMA	Time Division Multiple Access
TDOS	Tape Disk Operating System
TDR	Tape Data Register
TDR	Time Delay Relay
TDR	Tone Dial Receiver
TDR	Transmit Data Register
TDS	Transaction Data Set
TDS	Transaction Distribution System
TDS	Transaction Driven System
TE	Task Element
TE	Technical Engineer
TE	Terminal Equipment
TE	Text Editor
TEAM	Terminal Expandable Added Memory
tech	Technical
TEL	Task Execution Language
tel	Telephone
TEM	Test Equipment Manufacturing
temp	Temporary
TEP	Terminal Error Program
term	Terminal
test	Testament
tex	Telex
TF	Tape Feed
TF	Terminal Frame
TF	Transmit Filter
TG	Task Group
TG	Technology Gap
tg	Telegraph
TG	Terminator Group
TH	Transmission Header
TI	Tape Inverter
TI	Technical Information
TI	Technical Integration
TI	Terminal Instruction
TI	Terminal Interface
TI	Test Instrumentation
TIP	Terminal Interface Processor
TIQ	Task Input Queue
tit	Title
tkt	Ticket
TL	Total Load
TL	Transaction Language

TL	Transaction Listing
TL	Transmission Level
TL	Transmission Line
TLA	Telex Line Adapter
TLA	Time Line Analysis
TLA	Transmission Line Adapter
TLA	Transmission Line Assembly
TLP	Term Lease Plan
TLU	Table Look-Up
TM	Tape Mark
TM	Tape Module
TM	Test Mode
TM	Time Monitor
TM	Training Manual
TMP	Terminal Monitor Program
TMR	Triple Modular Redundancy
TN	Terminal Node
TN	Test Number
TN	Transport Network
TO	Technical Order
TO	Time Out
TO	Transmitter Order
to	Turnover
TOC	Table Of Contents
TOD	Time Of Day
TOS	Tape Operating System
tot	Total
TP	Technical Paper
tp	Teleprinter
TP	Terminal Point
TP	Terminal Printer
TP	Test Procedure
TP	Transaction Processor
TP	Transition Period
TPI	Tracks Per Inch
TPL	Terminal Programming Language
TPR	Technical Proposal Requirements
TR	Tape Resident
TR	Technical Report
TR	Test Request
TR	Test Run
tr	Translation
TR	Translation Register
TR	Trouble Report
TRACS	Traffic Reporting And Control System
TRC	Table Reference Character
TRE	Time Request Element
treas	Treasure
trf	Transfer

trk	Track
TRM	Test Request Message
TS	Technical Specification
TS	Telecommunication System
TS	Time Sharing
TS	Time Switch
TS	Transmission Service
TS	Transport Station
TS	Type Specification
TSAC	Time Slot Assignment Circuit
TSB	Terminal Status Block
TSC	Time Sharing Control
TSCB	Task Set Control Block
TSI	Test Structure Input
tsk	Task
TSO	Time Sharing Option
TSOS	Time Sharing Operating System
TSP	Time Series Processor
TSRT	Task Set Reference Table
TSS	Terminal Send Side
TSS	Time Sharing Service
TSS	Time Sharing System
tst	Test
TT	Technical Test
TT	Transaction Telephone
TT	Transaction Terminal
TT	Transmitting Typewriter
TTD	Temporary Text Delay
TTF	Terminal Transaction Facility
TU	Tape Unit
TU	Time Unit
TU	Transfer Unit
TU	Transmission Unit
TU	Transport Unit
TUR	Traffic Usage Recorder
TUT	Transistor Under Test
tv	Television
TV	Transfer Vector
TW	Time Word
tw	Typewriter
TWA	Transaction Work Area
TWS	Translator Writing Systems
TWT	Traveling Wave Tube
TWTA	Traveling Wave Tube Amplifier
tx	Telex
TXA	Terminal Exchange Area
typ	Typical

UADS	User Attribute Data Set
UART	Universal Asynchronous Receiver Transmitter
UBHR	User Block Handling Routine
UCA	Upper Control Area
UCC	Universal Commercial Code
UCC	Universal Copyright Convention
UCF	Utility Control Facility
UCS	Universal Character Set
UDC	Universal Decimal Classification
UDS	Universal Data Set
UE	Unit Equipment
UE	User Equipment
UF	Used For
UF	Utility File
UFP	Utility Facilities Program
UH	Unit Head
UH	Upper Half
UHF	Ultrahigh Frequency
UHL	User Header Label
UIO	Units In Operation
UL	Underwriters Laboratories
UL	Upper Limit
UL	User Language
ULA	Uncommitted Logic Array
ULC	Universal Logic Circuit
ULSI	Ultra Large Systems Integration
ult	Ultimately
unan	Unanimous
univ	Universal
up	Uniprocessor
UPC	Universal Product Code
UPL	User Programming Language
UPS	Uninterruptible Power Supply
UPS	Universal Processing System
URC	Unit Record Controller
US	Unit Separator
USAM	Unique Sequential Access Method
usu	Usually
UT	Unit Tester
UT	Universal Time
UTA	User Transfer Address
uti	Utility
UTL	User Trailer Label

VAB	Voice Answer-Back
vac	Vacancy
VAC	Value Added Carrier
VAC	Vector Analog Computer
VAI	Video Assisted Instruction
val	Value
VAM	Virtual Access Method
VAN	Value Added Network
var	Variable
var	Variety
VAT	Value Added Tax
VAT	Virtual Address Translator
VCBA	Variable Control Block Area
VCO	Voltage Control Oscillator
VCR	Valuation by Components Rule
VCR	Video Cassette Recorder
vd	Void
VDE	Variable Display Equipment
VDI	Video Display Interface
VDI	Video Display Input
VDI	Virtual Device Interface
VDI	Visual Display Input
VDP	Vertical Data Processing
VDP	Video Data Processor
VDP	Video Display Processor
VDU	Video Display Unit
VDU	Visual Display Unit
vert	Vertical
VF	Variable Factor
VF	Variable Frequency
VF	Video Frequency
VF	Visual Field
VF	Voice Frequency
VFC	Variable File Channel
VFC	Voltage Frequency Channel
VFU	Vertical Format Unit
VG	Vector Generator
VG	Voice Grade
VHF	Very High Frequency
VHLL	Very High Level Language
VHS	Video Home System
VICC	Visual Information Control Console
vid	Video

VIO	Very Important Object
VIO	Video Input/Output
VIO	Virtual Input/Output
VIP	Value In Performance
VIP	Variable Individual Protection
VIP	Vector Instruction Processor
VIP	Verifying Interpreting Punch
VIP	Versatile Information Processor
VIT	Very Intelligent Terminal
VL	Vector Length
VLDB	Very Large Data Base
VLF	Variable Length Field
VLF	Very Low Frequency
VLSI	Very Large Scale Integration
VLT	Video Layout Terminal
VM	Vertical Merger
VM	Virtual Machine
VM	Virtual Memory
VMA	Virtual Machine Assist
VME	Virtual Machine Environment
VMOS	Virtual Memory Operating System
VMS	Virtual Memory System
VMT	Virtual Memory Technique
VNL	Via Net Loss
vol	Volume
VOS	Virtual Operating System
VOS	Voice Operated Switch
VP	Vector Processor
VP	Verifying Punch
VP	Vertical Parity
VP	Virtual Processor
VPN	Virtual Page Number
VPU	Virtual Processing Unit
VR	Virtual Route
VR	Visible Record
VRAM	Variable Random Access Memory
VRC	Vertical Redundancy Check
VRC	Visible Record Computer
vs	Versus
VS	Virtual Storage
VS	Virtual System
VS	Vocal Synthesis
VSA	Value Systems Analysis
VSA	Visual Scene Analysis
VSAM	Virtual Storage Access Method
VSE	Virtual Storage Extended
VSM	Virtual Storage Management
VSN	Volume Serial Number
VSPX	Vehicle Scheduling Program Extended

VT	Vertical Tabulation
VT	Video Terminal
VT	Virtual Terminal
VTAM	Virtual Terminal Access Method
VTB	Video Terminal Board
VTC	Virtual Terminal Control
VTE	Visual Task Evaluation
VTI	Video Terminal Interface
VTOC	Volume Table Of Content
VTR	Video Tape Recording
VU	Voice Unit
VU	Volume Unit
VV	Vice Versa
VV	Volume in Volume
VZ	Virtual Zero

WAC	Working Address Counter
WACS	Wire Automated Check System
WADS	Wire Area Data Service
WAN	Wide Area Network
WAP	Work Assignment Procedure
WAR	With All Risks
WATS	Wide Area Telecommunications Service
WB	Write Buffer
WBS	Work Breakdown Structure
WC	Word Count
WC	Work Card
WC	Work Control
WC	Write Control
WCS	Work Control System
WCS	Writable Control Storage
WD	Wiring Diagram
WD	Work Description
WD	Work Directive
WD	Write Data
WDC	World Data Center
wdt	Width
WE	Write Enable
WI	Word Intelligibility
WIP	Work In Progress
wk	Week
WL	Word Line
WL	Work Level
WM	Work Mark

WO	Wait Order
wo	Without
WO	Write Only
WO	Write Out
WP	Word Processing
WP	Write Protection
WPM	Words Per Minute
WPS	Words Per Second
wr	Write
WRU	Who Are You?
ws	Worksheet
WT	Wait Time
WT	Walk Through
wt	Weight
WT	Word Terminal
WT	Word Type
WTO	Write-To-Operation
WTR	Work Transfer Record
WTR	Work Transfer Request
WU	Work Unit
WV	Weight in Volume
WV	Working Voltage
WW	Wire Wrap

XA	Auxiliary Amplifier
XAM	External Address Modifier
XBC	External Block Controller
XEC	Extended Emulator Control
XM	Expended Memory
XN	Execution Node
XR	External Request

YAP	Yield Analysis Pattern
yd	Yard
YEC	Youngest Empty Cell
YG	Yield Grade
YN	Yes-No
YOE	Year Of Entry
YP	Yield Point

YPS	Yards Per Second
yr	Year
YS	Yield Strength
YSF	Yield Safety Factor
YTC	Yield To Call

Z

ZA	Zero Adder
ZAI	Zero Address Instruction
ZB	Zero Bit
ZCR	Zero Crossing Rate
ZE	Zero Error
ZFC	Zero Failure Criteria
ZI	Zero Input
ZIP	Zone Improvement Plan
ZIP	Zone Information Protocol
ZO	Zero Output
ZOD	Zero Order Detector
ZOH	Zero Order Hold
ZPR	Zero Power Resistance
ZRE	Zero Rate Error
ZS	Zero Shift
ZSG	Zero Speed Generator
ZT	Zero Time
ZWC	Zero Word Count

Notes